THE LIQUIDATION/ MERGER ALTERNATIVE

THE LIQUIDATION/ MERGER ALTERNATIVE

by Michael J. Peel

BeardBooks
Washington, DC

Copyright© 1990 by Michael J. Peel
Reprinted 2003 by Beard Books, Washington, D.C.

Library of Congress Cataloging-in-Publication Data

Peel, Michael J., 1953-
   The liquidation/merger alternative / by Michael J. Peel
   p. cm.
   Originally published: Aldershot, Hants England ; Brookfield, Vt., USA :
Avebury, c1990.
   Includes bibliographical references and index.
   ISBN 1-58798-157-2 (pbk : alk, paper)
   1. Consolidation and merger of corporations. 2. Bankruptcy. 3. Business failures. I.
Title.

HD2746.5 .P44 2003
658.1'6--dc21

                                                                2002038407

Printed in the United States of America

THE LIQUIDATION/MERGER ALTERNATIVE

To Helga Maria

Contents

List of tables

Acknowledgements

I am indebted to a number of people who have made publication of this book possible. In particular, to Professor Richard Morris who kindly made available the Liverpool University Extel database for data collection; and to Nick Wilson, University of Bradford Management Centre, for many fruitful discussions during the period when the idea for the book was being formulated.

I would also like to thank Joyce Brown of the Cardiff Business School library for keeping me constantly updated with new references; Wendy Morgan for the cheerful way she single-handedly typed a difficult and demanding manuscript; Janet Peel for proof reading and indexing the book; and Helga Eckart for compiling the bibliography.

1 Introduction

Scope and aims of the book

Whereas a colossal amount has been written about the theory and rationale for mergers, but comparatively little on statistical models to predict these events, a mass of research has been directed towards the development of corporate failure prediction models, with relatively little effort expended on the development of a comprehensive theory of corporate collapse.

Between these two areas of research lies a third (but related) field of study, the bankruptcy/merger alternative; which, by comparison, has received scant attention in the literature - particularly in the domain of empirical research.

The bankruptcy/merger alternative is concerned with providing a rationale/theory as to why specific companies, which appear to be on the brink of corporate collapse, are nevertheless taken-over, rather than entering into receivership or liquidation. Only one previous US empirical study, by Pastena and Ruland (1986), has attempted to design statistical models with the aim of discriminating between those 'distressed' companies which fail, and those where a timely merger appears to serve as a viable alternative to corporate bankruptcy.

This book provides some new empirical evidence on the liquidation/merger alternative for the UK corporate sector. A number of statistical models are developed, with the aim of investigating whether it is possible to discriminate between 'distressed' acquired firms and ones that fail. The pioneering work of Pastena and Ruland is extended, both by increasing the explanatory variable set, and by attempting to discriminate simultaneously between three corporate outcomes: failure, non-failure, and distressed acquisition.

Chapter 2 provides a detailed review of the existing theory and evidence pertaining to the bankruptcy/merger alternative. Chapter 3 describes the data, methodology, sampling criteria and the variables employed to build the models. Chapter 4 presents the empirical results of the study, together with the classification accuracy of the various models.

Chapter 5 outlines some recent theoretical and applied work relating to mergers and acquisitions. Chapter 6 follows this with a review of recent developments in the corporate failure literature.

Chapter 7 ends the book with some concluding comments on the salient points to emerge from the study, together with suggested areas for future research.

The remainder of this chapter is devoted to describing the more general research relating to corporate failure and mergers, with the aim of 'setting the scene' for the more detailed analysis which follows.

Theory/causes of corporate failure

As has been noted by many researchers who have developed failure prediction models (e.g., Taffler, 1984; Storey, et. al., 1987), there is very little theoretical work underpinning these 'data-driven models'. The earliest work on the causes of corporate failure appears to emanate from the US.

Altman (1971) reported the results of a 1932 study, conducted by the Department of Commerce, which concluded that the major causes of corporate failure were: inefficient management, adverse domestic and personal factors, unwise extension of credit, and dishonesty and fraud.

Dewing (1941) thought there were four fundamental economic causes of corporate failure. These were:

2

(i) competitive forces, (ii) unprofitable expansion, (iii) cessation of public demand, and (iv) excess payment of capital charges. Altman (ibid., p. 55), in his own investigation of the aggregate economic reasons for US corporate failures, concluded that 'a firm's propensity to fail is heightened during periods of reduced economic growth, stock market performance and money supply conditions'.

Altman (1983) also reported the results of a 1980 Dunn and Bradstreet survey, which investigated the causal factors associated with the failure of 15,000 US businesses. The most striking result to emerge, was that the overwhelming cause of corporate failure was identified as 'managerial incompetence' - over 94 per cent of all failures were associated with managerial lack of experience, unbalanced experience, or 'plain incompetence'. The remaining causes were: neglect (0.8 per cent), fraud (0.5 per cent), and 'unknown' (3.5 per cent).

Ross and Kami (1973), in a major study of corporate failure, also concluded mismanagement was the key factor responsible for corporate collapse. They formulated a list of 'ten commandments' which management must not break if they want to avoid corporate failure. These included: all the Board must actively participate; and 'no one-man rule' - the latter being a point to emerge in most studies in this area. For example, Smith (1966), after analysing a number of business failures, concluded that the major causes of corporate collapse were: the autocratic manager, resistance to change, over-diversification, 'bad luck', lack of control, and decentralisation.

Bathory (1984), in his book on corporate collapse, developed a tripartite analysis of business failure. Here, he argues, corporate insolvency can be classified into three groupings - each with its own specific characteristics:

(a) acute insolvency: e.g., insufficient cash in the present or short term to meet financial obligations as they fall due;

(b) chronic insolvency: e.g., inability to meet financial obligations as they fall due over two or more accounting periods; and

(c) terminal insolvency: e.g., inability to fund 'more or less' permanent changes in the balance sheet.

3

In a more recent book devoted to corporate failure, Kharbanda and Stallworthy (1985) indicate four stages, or 'syndromes', of corporate failure: (i) impulse syndrome - 'running blind'; (ii) the stagnant bureaucracy; (iii) the 'headless' firm; and (iv) swimming upstream - taking 'sizeable risks'.

However, perhaps the best known work on the causes and symptoms of corporate decline is that articulated by Argenti (1976; 1983). Argenti considers that ratio analysis and failure prediction models are useful analytical tools only when failure is imminent; since these techniques analyse only the symptoms of corporate failure, and not the causes, which happen some years earlier.

Argenti's model of the causes of business failure is viewed in terms of a number of inherent defects in the organisational and financial structure of a firm which, in conjunction with business hazards and environmental change, lead down 'the long path to failure'. Three different paths are identified, but the main 'signal' is in the form of poor management - particularly the presence of an autocratic chief executive. Argenti (1983, p.77) concluded:

> To avoid failure, companies need to avoid three main defects: (1) autocratic chief executive, (2) poor accounting systems, (3) inadequate response to change. To rescue a company after it has travelled some years down the failure path, one may need to: (1) dismiss the chief executive, (2) reduce the company's gearing, (3) improve accounting systems, (4) modernise the old-fashioned.

Argenti also developed an 'A-score' method of 'forecasting' corporate failure, whereby points are assigned to 'clearly marked signposts, at least a dozen of them clearly marked' (e.g., autocratic chief executive-eight points; overtrading-fifteen points; 'creative' accounting-four points).

Although the work of Argenti and others offers an interesting attempt to provide a theory of corporate failure, these studies are essentially judgemental in nature, with no statistical basis and/or lack a concrete empirical foundation.

Chapter 6, inter alia, presents the results of a number of more recent studies which have attempted to empirically model the predictive content of the qualitative factors, identified by Argenti and others, as being important determinants of corporate collapse.

Failure prediction models

Since the seminal work of Altman (1968), a large number of researchers have developed multivariate statistical models, based mainly on financial ratios, with the aim of 'predicting' corporate collapse, as evidenced by corporate bankruptcy. Altman pioneered the application of Multiple Discriminant Analysis (MDA, see Chapter 3) to the dichotomous fail/non-fail corporate outcomes. Using a Z-score technique, his analysis was multivariate in nature, in that five 'traditional' financial ratios were combined in a linear discriminant function, with the aim of differentiating between failed and non-failed (solvent) firms. His model was able to successfully classify 95 per cent of the firms in his original sample.

To illustrate the huge proliferation of research in this area, just three recent articles are mentioned which review the evolution of corporate failure prediction models. Taffler (1984) refers to 13 UK failure prediction models developed over the period 1972 to 1983. Altman (1983), and Dambolena (1983), jointly refer to in excess of 50 models developed in the US over a similar period.

Excluding the US and the UK, Altman (1984) describes the development of over 25 failure prediction models, emanating from 10 different countries, ranging from Japan to Brazil. Since the publication of Altman's 1968 Z-score model, the classification accuracy claimed for these models has risen to 100 per cent, using data one year before failure; and as high as 98 per cent, employing data as far back as five years before failure (Taffler, 1984).

An early criticism of these 'claims' was forcefully enunciated by Johnson (1970, p.1168). He stated that such models were not 'truly' predictive in nature, since they required ex-post knowledge of failed companies. Thus, according to Johnson, all these models can really do is 'demonstrate that failed and non-failed firms have dissimilar ratios, not that ratios have predictive power'. Altman (1970, p.1170) countered:

The argument of ex-post rationalisation is hardly appropriate, since several completely new samples of firms were classified quite accurately, based on a model developed from different samples ... To conclude that a model consisting of financial ratios is 'largely descriptive, devoid of predictive content', is not only unfounded, but lacking in empirical support.

A further criticism of these models is that the non-failed samples are not randomly selected, but rather restricted to 'sound' or 'healthy' companies, and thus 'purged' of 'problematical firms' (see e.g., Taffler, 1984). Hence a problem common to 'traditional' two-group failure prediction models is that there appears to be a 'grey area' into which the classification of firms as failed or non-failed is indeterminate. This may be considered to be a particular weakness of existing models, since it might be perceived as being more helpful to the analyst - and a more robust test of the predictive power of the models - to correctly classify these grey area companies, rather than firms which more obviously fall into two discrete samples.

For example, the authors of a recent study (Peel and Peel, 1987), of 197 large private UK companies, found that their logit models, based on loss-making and failed firms, could not effectively discriminate between these two groups in validation samples - casting some doubt on the 'true' predictive content of 'traditional' models. The implications of this study are discussed further in Chapter 6.

Because it is 'well known' that conventional accounting data 'cannot capture all significant aspects of a firm's economic circumstances' (El Hennawy and Morris, 1983, p.111), recent efforts have been made to incorporate financial/qualitative variables into corporate failure models, in an attempt to improve their explanatory power. For example, a number of credit analysts (see Peel, 1985) have attested to the fact that firms in financial difficulties often delay publication of their annual reports and accounts (see Chapter 3).

In this respect Argenti (1983, p.68) has noted that 'the problem with Z-scores and ratios is that companies in trouble take care to delay publication of their accounts'.

Recent empirical research has shown that variables

measuring the timeliness of annual accounts are significant predictors of corporate failure, alone, or in combination with financial ratios: up to three years before failure for quoted firms (Peel, 1985); for large private companies (Peel, 1987); and for small private firms (Storey, et. al., 1987).

Other qualitative variables found to be significant predictors include: changes in the proportion of directors' resignations and appointments (Peel, Peel and Pope, 1985); changes in directors' shareholdings (Peel, et. al., 1986); and going concern qualifications, board size, and floating charges (Storey, et. al., 1987; Peel, 1989).

Other recent research (e.g., El Hennawy and Morris, 1983a) suggests that a combination of share price residuals with financial and non-financial variables, may improve the explanatory power and reliability of failure prediction models. The implications of these studies are analysed more comprehensively in Chapter 6.

The causes of mergers: theory

Because of the huge body of literature in this field (see e.g., Cosh, et. al., 1984), at this stage only the key theories are outlined. A more comprehensive review of recent developments is given in Chapter 5.

Financial economies

Many theories have focused on the derived economic/financial economies as being the prime rationale for takeovers. Mueller (1977) reviews a number of these, which broadly classify the economies as follows:

(a) Leverage: because borrowing costs reduce with firm size, larger companies can refinance the debt of small firms at lower cost - resulting in a 'genuine' capital gain.

(b) Diversification: the pooling of imperfectly correlated income streams will produce a superior risk/return asset compared to the individual streams.

(c) 'P/E magic': here the rationale is that if one firm acquires another with a lower P/E ratio, the

7

market may value the joint earnings of the two firms at the higher P/E of the acquirer; and 'thus producing an instantaneous capital gain'.

(d) <u>Growth-resource mismatch</u>: this hypothesis (see e.g., Palepu, 1986, p. 17) states that high-growth, resource-poor, firms may make attractive acquisition targets. This is 'suggested by recent literature which analyses the investment and finance decisions of firms under asymmetric information'.

(e) <u>Gort's economic disturbance theory</u>: Gort (1969, p.17) posits that mergers may be explained by 'economic disturbances', which involve a 'discrepancy between the value of a firm's assets placed on it by managers or controlling stockholders, and the value placed on it by outsiders'.

(f) <u>M-form redeployment of corporate capital</u>: this structure of divisionalized organisation enables central management, following a takeover: 'to move capital from high average return, low marginal, divisions to those promising the highest marginal returns without undergoing the transactions costs of using the capital market'.

(g) <u>Removal of incompetent</u> managers: Manne (1965) introduced a theory of 'the market for corporate control', whereby:

> firms compete for control of inefficiently managed companies ... mergers are seen as an economical way of eliminating bad management, reorganizing corporate structures, and improving both allocational, and X, efficiency in the corporate sector.

Finally Hughes, et. al., (1984, p.27), after reviewing the determinants of mergers, concluded:

> the most frequently hypothesized causes of mergers are to bring about an increase in profits by either increasing the market power of the firm or reducing its costs or both. Market power may be increased by merger, either by affecting the elasticity of demand for the

firm's products or raising barriers to entry.

Other theories

A number of authors, particularly in the business policy literature, focus on the strategic rationale relating to corporate acquisition. Johnson and Scholes (1984, p.197), for example, are of the opinion that the 'most compelling' reason for acquisition is the speed of development it facilitates into new product/industrial areas. Another common reason being:

> the lack of knowledge or resources to develop strategies internally. For example, a company may be acquired for its R & D expertise, or its knowledge of property speculation, or a particular type of production system.

Weston and Mansinghka (1971, p.928) introduced a 'defensive diversification' hypothesis:

> Analysis of the backgrounds and acquisition histories of conglomerate firms suggested that they were diversifying defensively to avoid: (1) sales and profit stability, (2) adverse growth developments, (3) adverse competitive shifts, (4) technological obsolescence, and (5) increased uncertainties associated with their industries.

Ansoff (1965) has noted that 'synergy' is an important motive for mergers, otherwise known as the "2+2=5" effect. This is a commonly quoted rationale for unrelated diversification; that is, where two or more activities or processes complement each other, such that the combined effect 'is greater than the sum of its parts'. These synergies may be in the areas of finance, management, marketing, investment or production.

Mandelker (1974, p.306) has also outlined an 'abnormal gains' hypothesis, which overlaps with some of the previously mentioned theories:

this hypothesis states that information concerning a forthcoming acquisition is generally considered 'good' news for the acquiring firm. These include economies of scale, attainment of monopoly, or economic power that stems from bigness, undervalued securities, diversification, improvements of the marketability of stocks, and others.

Finally, managerial theories argue that the separation of corporate ownership from control enables directors to pursue goals other than the maximisation of stockholders' welfare (profit). For example, the pursuit of growth ('empire building'), or a 'speculative or risk-taking motive', via the vehicle of takeover. In contrast, Harvey (1963) provides a list of managerial motives for making acquisitions which do attempt to maximise shareholders' welfare. These include: (1) market motivation e.g., capturing increased market share or 'completing' a product line, (ii) utilization of excess liquidity, (iii) acquisition of key personnel skills, and (iv) distribution economies, diversification, and combined research and development.

The rationale for mergers: evidence

Newbould (1970), in an early study of 1967/68 UK takeovers, discovered that the so called 'text book' reasons for mergers (technological, economic, synergic, financial, and industrial reorganisation), accounted for only eighteen per cent of the motivating factors managers gave for acquisitions. In fact, 'market dominance' (27 per cent) and 'defensive' strategies (21 per cent) were found to be primary motivating factors.

Cosh, et. al., (1984, p.267), in a more recent study of takeovers between 1967 and 1969, provide a univariate analysis of the characteristics of 290 acquired and non-acquired quoted companies. Their results, based on a comparison of the mean values of a number of financial ratios: 'did not yield evidence in support of there being any one single dominant motive for merger'. No evidence was found in support of Gort's disturbance theory; but the authors did discover that merging firms were, on average, much larger than non-merging firms:

this does not imply that mergers do not take place for reasons of economies of scale. All it does suggest is that the latter is unlikely to be an overriding or the single dominant motive for mergers (ibid., p.249).

Cosh, et. al., also reported that acquiring firms had significantly higher pre-merger leverage ratios than acquired firms: 'with some evidence to suggest that firms may be seeking merger partners with dissimilar leverage ratios to their own'. Finally, based on variations in profit ratios, the authors found some evidence to indicate that risk-spreading may be a motive for mergers.

Mueller (op.cit., p.339), following his review of eight independent empirical studies over the period 1970 to 1976, concluded that:

mergers result in no net gain to the firm's stockholders...but the evidence is broadly consistent with the hypothesis that managers pursue corporate growth or other objectives that are not directly related to stockholder welfare and economic efficiency.

However, Mueller (ibid., p.326) noted in relation to the returns to acquired company shareholders:

Every study which has examined the benefits (to acquired company stockholders)...has found that the stockholders of the acquired firms earn significantly higher rates of return on their shares, than other shares are earning, both over the immediate period before the merger and including a reasonable period after the merger is consummated.

This statement is certainly supported by Jensen and Ruback (1983, p.15) who, after reviewing the evidence of 13 independent empirical studies over the period 1977 to 1983, on target firm stockholder returns, concluded:

The evidence indicated that the targets of

11

successful tender offers and mergers, earn significantly positive abnormal returns on announcement of the offers and through completion of the offers. Targets of unsuccessful tender offers earn significantly positive abnormal returns on the offer announcement and through the realisation of failure.

Hence, evidence on the so called 'unhappy marriage' (Meeks, 1977), between targets and acquiring firms, appears to follow a productive honeymoon period, at least for one partner - stockholders of the acquired firm.

Takeover prediction models

In comparison with the huge number of failure prediction models reported in recent years, models developed to predict takeover targets have been relatively scarce. This is somewhat surprising, given the investment implications (abnormal returns) associated with correctly identifying acquisition targets (see Jensen and Ruback, 1983).

Empirical studies, by Stevens (1973); Belkaoui (1978); Rege (1984); and Palepu (1986), refer jointly to about ten previous attempts to develop acquisition models. In general, these models are - like failure prediction models - based on matched samples of acquired and non-acquired firms; are usually based on accounting information one year prior to aquisition; predominantly employ 'conventional' financial ratios; and, bar one, rely on the statistical technique of discriminant analysis (see Chapter 3).

Although the methodology is similar to that employed in failure prediction models, the explanatory power and classification accuracy of takeover prediction models is generally much lower. Belkaoui (op. cit., p.104) reports an overall classification rate of 84 per cent for his estimation sample, rising to 85 per cent in validation samples. Generally, however, the reported classification accuracy of these published models is somewhat lower.

One of the earliest attempts to develop a takeover prediction model was made by Stevens (1973). Using discriminant analysis on a sample of 40 firms acquired in 1966, matched by size with 40 non-acquired firms, he discovered that financial ratios measuring leverage and liquidity were statistically significant predictors between the samples. His results suggested that, relative to non-acquisition targets, acquired firms had lower leverage and higher liquidity ratios. However, Stevens found no significant differences between the samples on the basis of profitability ratios. His model was able to predict only seventy per cent of the acquisition targets in his original sample.

Belkaoui (1978) developed a later model based on 25 Canadian listed companies which were acquired over the period 1960 to 1968. These were matched by size with 25 non-acquired firms. A validation sample of 11 acquired and 11 non-acquired firms was used to assess the predictive ability of the models.

His 'best' model was based on data three years before acquisition, and had an overall classification accuracy of 84 and 85 per cent, respectively, in his original and validation samples. Belkaoui's derived discriminant function contained no less than 16 different financial ratios. In consequence, he made no attempt to assess the relative contribution of each ratio to the model's (apparent) explanatory power.

In contrast to the empirical findings of Belkaoui, Rege (1984), in a more recent Canadian study, reported that his discriminant model was unable to differentiate, on the basis of five 'traditional' financial ratios, between acquired and non-acquired firms. Rege's study was the first to report such a result. His findings tended to suggest that the apparent explanatory power of earlier models may have been sample-specific.

The most comprehensive study to date on predicting takeover targets has recently been reported by Palepu (1986). His results are particularly interesting since: (i) the samples are much larger than have been employed in previous research; and (ii) the variables are specified on the basis of six 'frequently suggested' merger hypotheses. Palepu's estimation sample comprised 163 US listed manufacturing companies which had been acquired over the period 1971 to 1977, together with a random sample of 256 non-acquired manufacturing concerns.

The predictive ability of his logit models (see Chapter 3) was tested on validation samples of 30 acquired and 1,087 non-acquired firms. The statistically significant variables in his models suggested that managerial inefficiency, growth-resource imbalance, and smaller size, were all likely to increase the probability of a firm becoming a takeover target. In addition, takeover targets were more likely to be characterised by relatively low growth and low leverage.

However, Palepu found no significant differences between acquired and non-acquired firms on the basis of 'merger' variables, suggested as theoretically appropriate; that is, price-earnings ratios, return on equity, and liquiditiy ratios. Although Palepu did not report the within-sample classification accuracy of his model, it was able to correctly classify 24 (80 per cent) of the 30 acquired firms, but only 486 (45 per cent) of the 1087 non-acquired companies, in his validation samples (overall accuracy: 46 per cent). Hence, compared to previous studies, and on the basis of a population representative sampling base, 'the model cannot predict targets accurately'.

Another interesting feature of Palepu's research was his investigation of whether it was possible, using his model, to earn abnormal returns by investing in the stocks of 'predicted' takeover targets. His results, derived from daily stock prices, led him to conclude that:

> the strategy of investing in 625 firms identified by the model to be potential targets is found to result in statistically insignificant excess returns. Hence, the estimated model's ability to predict targets is not superior to that of the stock market (ibid., p.37).

The empirical findings of Palepu are the most important in this field to date. This is for two major reasons. The first relates to the statistical vigour of his research. The methodological flaws of previous studies - such as non-random equal-sized samples, and arbitrary cut-off points - were corrected for. Secondly, his finding that the predictive ability of his model was not superior to that of the stock market, throws some doubt on the validity of the claims of previous model builders, that they can accurately predict takeover targets up to five years before acquisition.

To significantly improve the explanatory power of

takeover prediction models probably lies, as noted by Carleton, et. al., (1983, p.833) in the extension of the modelling technique to include acquiring firms:

Such complex phenomena ultimately depend on characteristics of both acquiring and acquired firms. As a result, traditional empirical work that simply categorizes firms as acquired or non-acquired may not detect the nature of merger pairings, since such categorization is only capable of determining the average effect that an acquired firm characteristic has on the likelihood of acquisition.

Summary

This chapter has outlined the scope and structure of the book, with particular emphasis on the empirical work which follows in Chapters 3 and 4. The remainder of the chapter was devoted to summarising the key developments, both theoretical and empirical, in the separate evolution of the theories of mergers and corporate failure. A review of the efficacy of statistical models which aim to predict these separate events, was also presented.

The chapter also emphasised how the two research areas of mergers and corporate failure have developed, almost exclusively, along separate lines.

The next chapter presents the (limited) existing theory and evidence pertaining to the bankruptcy/merger alternative. In comparison to the mass of empirical research devoted individually to mergers and corporate failure, a paucity of evidence currently exists in this relatively new field of research.

2 Existing theory and evidence

Introduction

Having considered in Chapter 1 the general theory and evidence pertaining to corporate failure and mergers, together with the efficacy of statistical models to predict these events, this chapter focuses on the limited theory and evidence relating to the bankruptcy/merger alternative, which links these two, what have previously been considered to be unrelated areas, together.

The bankruptcy/merger alternative (theory and evidence) is concerned with explaining the rationale for the acquisition of failing firms; and whether it is possible to discriminate, employing statistical models, between those distressed firms which fail and those where a timely merger appears to serve as a viable alternative to liquidation or receivership (failure). An example of the latter is provided by Steiner (1969, p.136):

A company may get into financial difficulties, as did the Douglas Aircraft Company in 1967, and merge with another one having the financial resources to provide the needed assistance.

One distinguished author (Mueller, 1977, p.334), after reviewing the empirical evidence on the effects of mergers, stated as recently as 1977 that 'no evidence has been gathered to suggest that acquired firms were to any degree in danger of bankruptcy'. Hence, much of the evidence considered in this chapter is of the conventional 'wisdom' variety, or provides 'weak' empirical support only.

However, two more recent US studies, by Shrieves and Stevens (1979), and Pastena and Ruland (1986), do provide more rigorous evidence; the former on the existence and extent of the 'bankruptcy avoidance' rationale for mergers; the latter on the predictive ability of statistical models designed to discriminate between financially distressed firms which fail, and those which appear to make attractive acquisition targets.

Furthermore, the acquisition of 'failing' firms has been recognized as an important aspect of US antitrust laws; whereby under the 'failing company doctrine', an otherwise illegal merger may be permitted if one of the companies is in 'imminent' danger of collapse. No empirical evidence on these issues is currently available for the UK corporate sector. Chapters 3 and 4 outline some new evidence for the UK on the liquidation/merger alternative.

Conventional wisdom and empirical evidence

Until the statement of Dewey (1961, p. 257), made during his discussion on US cartel policy, little attention had been paid to the fact that many companies, which might otherwise fail, are in fact taken-over. Dewey emphasised that:

> Most mergers, of course, have virtually nothing to do with either the creation of market power or the realization of scale economies. They are merely a civilized alternative to bankruptcy, or voluntary liquidation, that transfers assets from falling to rising firms.

Later evidence proved that Dewey was wrong to claim that most mergers were 'civilized' alternatives to failure. Notwithstanding this, however, his comments did stimulate much debate (and subsequent research). Manne (1965, p.112), for

17

example, pointed out that Dewey's argument was only a partial redemption of mergers, since it was limited to those cases in which bankruptcy or liquidation was imminent; in that 'the function so successfully performed by bankruptcies would be more economically performed by mergers at a much earlier stage of the firm's life'. Manne also postulated the idea of a market for corporate control, in which companies compete for the control of inefficiently managed resources (firms) via takeovers.

To empirically test the theories of Dewey and Manne, Boyle (1970) examined the accounts of 165 'large' US firms which were acquired between 1948 and 1968. He discovered that only 10 per cent were losing money in the year prior to acquisition. So, by equating loss-making firms with those which are likely to fail, Boyle (ibid., p. 169) concluded:

A careful examination of the facts showed that less than 10 per cent of large corporations which have been acquired over the past 20 years have been at 'death's door'. Have the large number of mergers we have witnessed over the past 20 years represented a response to actual or impending bankruptcy? The facts show that, with major exceptions, the answer is clear. No.

However Shrieves and Stevens (1979, p. 504) drew attention to the fact that Boyle's work was 'worth discussing in an important respect: his error in concluding that because impending bankruptcy did not play a role in most mergers, it is not a motive for mergers'. A further criticism of Boyle's study is that, by limiting his sample to 'large' acquired firms, he effectively excluded a potentially important group of 'small' acquired companies, some of which may have been acutely financially distressed. Indeed, the new empirical evidence presented in this book shows that both failed and 'distressed' acquired UK quoted companies were, on average, significantly smaller than a random sample of quoted firms (see Chapters 3 and 4).

In a more recent paper Conn (1976) suggested that there were two identifiable versions of the 'failing firm/industry doctrine'. Firstly a healthy firm may wish to acquire a failing firm, or one in a less profitable industry, for short-term financial benefits, such as the failing firm's tax-loss carryforward and appreciation of reported earnings per share. Conn described the second version in terms of acquisition being the quickest method of corporate diversification: 'which allows for the survival of the declining firm and results in instantaneous growth'.

However, Steiner (1969, p.652), in his book on corporate strategy, adds a warning note:

> Some companies look for others in distress with the hope of adding something to the combination that will correct a deficiency and revitalize an ailing enterprise. With few exceptions, these integrations do not work out much better than the situation of the girl who marries a man, to reform him.

Conn (op.cit., p.147), in order to test Dewey's claim that most acquired firms are 'failing', evaluated the profitability characteristics of 56 acquiring firms, and the firms they acquired, over the period 1960 to 1969. Using paired-difference statistical tests, Conn concluded that no support could be found for the failing firm/industry hypothesis:

> Firms of similar profitability, and similar profitability trends, merge ... First the acquired firms are not faltering. Second, the industries of the acquired firms are not faltering. The financial vitality of acquirers, and their respective industries, casts considerable doubt on the failing firm/industry defenses for conglomerate mergers.

Although Conn's work disproved Dewey's earlier claim, that most mergers are merely civilised alternatives to failure, it did not, like Boyle's previous study, disprove the hypothesis that some mergers fall into this category.

It is interesting to note that Johnson (1970, p.1116) criticised the 'predictive ability' of Altman's 1968 failure prediction model, because:

> While ratios do provide information about the

current status of the firm, they do not contain information about the alternative strategies and the intervening economic conditions confronting managers and investors, such as mergers.

Altman, (1970, p.1169), in replying to Johnson's criticism, concluded:

> While it is obviously true that alternative strategies, e.g. mergers, may avert a formal bankruptcy situation, this aspect does not diminish the overall usefulness of the ratio model ... If a company's management is able to recognise a potential dismal future through the analysis of ratios, alternatives may then be explored and bankruptcy possibly avoided.

So far, the evidence reviewed in this section relates exclusively to the US. In contrast, UK evidence is very thin. Johnson and Scholes (1984, p.192), in their book on corporate strategy, do mention that the 'overall cost of developing by acquisition may, in certain circumstances, be particularly advantageous. Companies going into liquidation may be a good buy'. However, Steiner (1983, p.241), in discussing merger strategies, offers contrary advice: 'do not acquire a company in distress'.

Slatter (1984, p. 272), in his book on turnaround strategies, gives the subject a fuller treatment. In describing why one large manufacturing company went into decline through acquisition strategy, Slatter noted that 'nearly all these (acquired) companies were failing or losing money at the time of acquisition'. In referring to the acquisition of 'losers' (firms which have no competitive advantages, have obsolete products, or have inferior cost positions), Slatter stated: 'when a firm with a weak competitive position is acquired, the new company becomes a cash drain. Having just purchased, management throws good money after bad in the hope of justifying their acquisition decisions. The sunk cost argument escapes them'. Slatter (ibid., p.97) also highlighted the dangers inherent in pursuing a strategy of acquiring failing firms for turnaround:

If management has once been successful in pulling a firm out of crisis ... it may take on a false sense of belief in its own abilities to turnaround acquired firms. PMA Holdings provides a good example of a firm that was headed for turnaround success when it foolishly acquired the furniture manufacturer Harris Lebus, when the latter was close to receivership. As an independent entity Harris Lebus was in a non-recoverable situation. The acquisition, coupled with the cyclical drop in demand due to the 1980/1981 recession, sent PMA itself into receivership in 1981.

Researchers who have developed UK failure prediction models have also made explicit reference to acquisition as an alternative strategy to liquidation. For example, Taffler (1984, p.219), in commenting on the performance of his discriminant failure prediction model, stated:

> In the three years subsequent to its development, there were 11 distribution company failures on EXSTAT with failure defined as receivership (4) acquisition as a clear alternative to bankruptcy (3) or rescue re-financing (4). In each case the company had an at risk profile on the basis of its last set of accounts.

In other words, of the 11 distribution quoted firms identified by the Taffler model as failing, three (27 per cent) were actually 'distressed' acquisitions. Furthermore, Tisshaw (1976, p. 203) reported similar findings for large UK private companies. He drew attention to the difficulties in defining private company failure because 'many companies that do fail disguise the failure by either being taken-over, amalgamating, reconstructing or changing in some other way'. As is argued in Chapter 3, this is an erroneous approach, since the acquisition of a financially distressed firm is an entirely different economic outcome from corporate failure - and one of much interest to analysts, shareholders and creditors - in terms of the positive and negative (potential) abnormal returns, respectively, associated with an a

<u>priori</u> investment decision (see e.g., Clark and Weinstein, 1983; Jensen and Ruback, 1983).

The regression syndrome

Vance (1971, p.22), who studied the 'top' 500 American industrial firms over the period 1954 to 1967, noted that only 13 had actually failed. He commented:

> Although the disappearance of bankruptcies from big business could be interpreted as a compliment to our prosperity, it can also mean that companies in relative difficulty prefer to merge rather than undergo bankruptcy. If so, this could have positive connotations: the defeated firms are not destroyed through dissolution, rather they are absorbed and rebuilt by more aggressive firms.

Vance, borrowing an analogy from the medical field - where the regression syndrome is the concurrence of several simultaneous symptoms - describes it as a 'fairly promising index of impending merger, name change, or, worst of all, dissolution'. The 'affliction' is evidenced by the economic deterioration of the business enterprise: 'among the more obvious of the syndrome's symptoms is a relative decline in sales, a deteriorating profit pattern, a shrinking labour force, and slow or no growth in owners' equity'. Vance ranked Fortune's top 500 American industrial firms according to several performance criteria. He discovered that in the ten year period prior to acquisition, the average fall in sales ranking experienced by three acquisition targets amounted to 119 places; for total assets (size), a decline of 129 places; for net income (profit), a decline of 97 places; and for size of workforce, a fall of 155 places.

Vance claimed that the regression syndrome was not confined to a few 'highly publicized examples'. He stated it was an 'almost universal manifestation'. He attempted to demonstrate this by analysing the entire population of firms in Fortune's 500. He noted that over the decade before acquisition, the sales performance of takeover targets ranged from a gain of 83 positions to a loss of 408, with the ratio of losers to gainers in the order of ten to one. Vance concluded that acquisition targets subject to the regression syndrome exhibit growth in annual sales and assets at only one-fifth the rate of non-merging firms.

Net income for non-merging firms increased at double the rate recorded for acquired companies. However, Vance (ibid., p.40) drew attention to manpower loss as the most 'obvious' index of decline:

> Although the large non-merging firms have boosted employment by about 3 per cent annually, the merger-prone regression syndrome firms actually decline by almost 3 per cent ... these statistics are probably less significant for their arithmetical accuracy than for their definite confirmation of the regression syndrome. On the basis of these data, it seems legitimate to infer that a firm in a chronic slump is a highly likely prospect for merger.

Although Vance's regression syndrome work is an interesting (and early) attempt to isolate the financial characteristics of large US acquisition targets, the validity of his conclusions is open to doubt, due to the lack of statistical significance testing in his study. Also, the omission of a control sample of failed firms from his analysis places his conclusions in the more 'generalised variety'.

However, it is interesting to note, in relation to Vance's observations on regression syndrome acquisition targets being characterised by a declining workforce, that the new empirical evidence in this book (Chapters 3 and 4), for UK quoted companies in the 1970's, supports his general conclusions. In the year prior to acquisition, a sample of 32 distressed acquired firms reduced their workforce by an average of five per cent. For a similar sample of 40 failed firms, the reduction amounted to three per cent; and for a control sample of 40 non-failed/non-acquired firms, there was an average yearly increase approaching two per cent.

Employing a Student's t-test, there was no significant difference (at the 5 per cent confidence level) between the mean workforce reduction of the failed and the distressed acquired firms. But both samples had significantly different mean changes in employees (a fall) from the non-failed control sample (a rise). Hence for the UK corporate sector, in the 1970's at any rate, it appears that both financially distressed firms which failed, or were acquired, reduced their workforces significantly in the year before acquisition/failure. However, the mean percentage reduction in workforce, of failing and distressed acquired companies, did not differ significantly.

Mergers and the failing company doctrine

Under US antitrust laws, a defence to merger prosecution has evolved which is known as the 'failing company doctrine'. The doctrine dates back to a 1930 Supreme Court judgement, in the case of International Shoe versus the Federal Trade Commission. It provides that two companies may be permitted to complete an otherwise illegal merger if it can be proved that one of the two companies would otherwise enter into corporate bankruptcy.

The rationale behind the doctrine is that the likely harm to communities, creditors, owners and employees, associated with a company which is in imminent danger of being liquidated, outweighs the potential harm to competition associated with allowing the failing company to be acquired (Blum, 1974). An obvious problem faced by the Supreme Court, and one subsequently debated by many professional and academic commentators (see Bok, 1960) , is in deciding when an acquisition target is actually failing. In the International Shoe case, the Supreme Court merely stated that the acquisition target should be a 'corporation with resources so depleted that it faced the grave probability of a business failure'. Subsequent judicial pronouncements have attempted to clarify the criteria upon which 'failure' is based. These include events signifying that a firm is on the 'verge' of bankruptcy/insolvency, such as entrance into a bankruptcy proceeding, inability to pay debts as they fall due, and an explicit agreement with creditors to reduce debts (Blum, op.cit.).

Based on a number of judicial decisions and Congressional reports, Sotiroff (1963, p.583) attempted to formulate a 'balancing test' for the failing company doctrine; whereby the apparent injury to competition would be weighed against the

probability of counteracting injury to those
involved with the failing firm:

> A court would balance such factors as the state
> of decline of the firm, the efforts expended by
> the firm to obtain other offers, the number of
> bids made, the difference in bids, and the
> difference between the lower bids and that
> amount likely to be realised if the failing
> company were forced to sell at a distress sale.

Altman (1983), in a 'non-comprehensive survey',
noted that between 1950 and 1978, seventeen
companies had invoked the failing company doctrine
as an explicit defence to merger prosecution under
US antitrust laws. In only four instances was the
defence successfully pleaded and the merger allowed
to proceed. Altman (ibid., p.239) commented that
'in most of these cases, anti-competitive
consequences were the evident basis of the decision,
and rarely, if ever, did the court articulate the
trade-off in costs'.

The failing company doctrine stimulated efforts
amongst researchers to develop statistical models
designed to predict corporate failure (e.g., Blum,
1974). According to Taffler (op.cit., p.237), since
1967 Z-score failure prediction models have been
utilized by the antitrust courts as an aid to
establishing the failing company doctrine. He
concluded:

> There is a potential for future use of models of
> business failure in certain areas of decision-
> making where legal issues are at stake, such as
> the failing company doctrine ... It may even be
> possible one day for the Antitrust Division, the
> Federal Trade Commission, and other government
> agencies to incorporate a model of business
> failure and a probabilistic decision rule into
> administrative determinants, such as issuing
> letters of clearance for proposed business
> combinations.

It is interesting to note that under UK monopoly
and merger legislation, there is no reported
instance of a ruling where the failing company

doctrine has been raised. However, the legislation, as presently framed, would appear to allow such a defence - since under Section 84 of the 1973 Fair Trading Act, the Monopolies and Mergers Commission, in deciding whether a proposed merger operates against the public interest, may take into account 'all relevant circumstances'. In any event, the 'spirit' of the failing company doctrine appears to be (implicitly) active in the UK. This is illustrated by the recent News International take-over of the Today newspaper, when the Trade and Industry Secretary decided not to refer the bid to the Monopolies and Mergers Commission because, if he had, the 'bid would have been withdrawn and the paper - which was sustaining losses of £500,000 per week - closed; with the loss of 500 jobs' (Guardian, 2 July, 1987).

Bankruptcy avoidance and mergers

Shrieves and Stevens (1979, p.501) noted that 'the bankruptcy avoidance motive is perhaps the most recently articulated of all merger motives, and perhaps the only one for which no systematic attempts at empirical validation have been forthcoming'. Their study presented evidence relating to the existence and extent of the bankruptcy avoidance motive for mergers in the US between 1948 and 1971. The origins of the rationale date back to the theoretical work of Lewellen (1971), who posited a 'pure financial rationale' for mergers where earning streams are less than perfectly correlated. His argument was based on the premise that the combined debt capacity of two firms, individually, was less than the debt capacity of a new entity resulting from their merger.

Lee and Barker (1977, p.1463), in discussing the mean-variance asset pricing model, introduced the concept of transaction costs relating to 'crisis' and bankruptcy possibilities on a firm's value. They described conditions of optimal firm debt capacity and attempted to illustrate: (a) that the optimal debt capacity for a merged firm exceeds the combined debt capacity of the unmerged firms, and (b) that under 'all states of nature', the costs of bankruptcy crises for a merged firm are less than, or equal to, the joint costs of unmerged firms:

The act of merging can properly be viewed as
having a direct and indirect effect on firm
value. The direct effect comes from the
avoidance of bankruptcy costs and a reduction in
the probability of bankruptcy at pre-merger debt
levels. Additionally, there is a gain in
aggregate firm value arising from the increase
in debt capacity for the post-merger firm.

The Shrieves and Stevens study addresses the role
of this 'direct effect', as well as articulating the
costs which merger avoids, including:
(i) the lower legal and administrative costs of
merger versus liquidation;
(ii) possible tax-loss carry-overs;
(iii) going-concern value in a merger is higher than
liquidation value;
(iv) the adverse effects of potential bankruptcy/
receivership on sales and cash flow, in consequence
of falling confidence of suppliers and customers;
and
(v) critical managerial talent may be less
predisposed to 'abandon ship' (see e.g., Peel, Peel
and Pope, 1986) if merger rather than failure is
perceived as imminent.
Shrieves and Stevens (ibid., p.504) point out that
because there is no systematic research on the
magnitude and extent of bankruptcy costs, and the
savings realised by merger, as an alternative to
liquidation, then:

Such an analysis would prove a relatively
unattractive venture. Thus our strategy in
exploring the possibility of bankruptcy
avoidance as a motive for merger, is to focus on
the incidence of distressed firms among firms
which have been acquired.

Their empirical findings were based on a
statistical comparison of two samples of large
manufacturing firms. The first consisted of 112
companies which were acquired during the period 1948
to 1971. The second comprised 112 non-acquired
firms which were matched by asset size, industrial
classification, and year, to the acquired companies.
Shrieves and Stevens suggested that if the
bankruptcy cost avoidance merger rationale was

supported, the relative frequency of firms likely to experience liquidation in the sample of acquired firms should be significantly higher than would be found in a randomly paired sample of non-acquired ones. To test this hypothesis, Altman's (1968) failure prediction model was applied to each sample of firms to identify those in 'danger' of failure. The model 'predicted' seventeen (15 per cent) of the acquired firms as failure candidates, with only five (5 per cent) of the non-acquired firms similarly predicted as 'failures'.

Hence the 'predicted' failure rate within the acquired sample of firms (15 per cent) was significantly higher than for both the actual failure rate of all companies (0.1 to 3 per cent); and also the 'predicted' failure rate (5 per cent) in the control sample of non-acquired matched firms. The authors (ibid., p.513) concluded:

> Whilst we have not attempted to ascertain the extent to which conditions of financial distress are correlated with economic and financial circumstances consistent with merger motives, our findings should provide valuable insights for further attempts of characterisation of acquired firms, and to the development of a more complete theory of mergers. An empirical corollary to our findings is that many instances of financial crisis are resolved through merger processes. To the extent that this process contributed to the efficiency with which resources are allocated to more productive ends, mergers serve a valuable function in our economy.

The empirical results of Shrieves and Stevens certainly support the contention that a significant proportion (15 per cent) of large manufacturing acquired firms in the US do appear to have financial characteristics which closely resemble those of firms which eventually fail. It is interesting to note, however, that those acquired firms predicted by Altman's model as failing are technically Type II errors (misclassification of a non-failed firm as failed). This leads naturally to the question: is it possible to discriminate between firms which are acquired but predicted as failing, and those companies which actually do fail? The empirical work of Pastena and Ruland seeks to address this question.

Bankruptcy/merger models

Pastena and Ruland (1986) made the first empirical attempt to model the bankruptcy/merger alternative with reference to variables largely based on ownership/control theory. Their study is concerned with conditions under which a merger appears to be an attractive alternative to liquidation:

> The distressed firm should be able to find a merger partner at some price as long as the net asset value is positive and under the assumption of a well functioning market for information. As the situation deteriorates towards a condition of negative net asset value, the possibility of merger is reduced (p.290).

Pastena and Ruland outlined the a priori rationale for incorporating a number of variables into their empirical models; that is, ownership concentration, gearing, size, and tax carryforwards.

Ownership concentration

This is measured as the total percentage of voting stock owned by managers, directors and 'other parties'. Pastena and Ruland (p.292) posit that a high concentration ratio implies owner rather than manager control and is therefore 'expected to be associated with the merger option. Low concentration implies a high degree of management control and should be associated with the bankruptcy alternative'.

The existing literature certainly suggests that shareholders of target firms should always prefer merger to bankruptcy, since in bankruptcy equity value frequently falls to zero (Clarke and Weinstein, 1983); whereas in a takeover, shareholders in the target firm receive shares and/or cash from the acquiring company, and frequently benefit from positive abnormal returns (Jensen and Ruback, 1983).

Hence, Pastena and Ruland's rationale for this variable is based upon the premise that, although unsecured creditors and shareholders of a failing firm would prefer merger, top managers may feel that their interests are better served through bankruptcy. The reasons proffered for this view were:

(a) managers of acquired firms lose power, prestige and the value of organisation-specific human capital;

(b) management may resist tender-offers because of their preference for control to preserve jobs, perquisites and any agency costs they are appropriating; and

(c) the results of an empirical study by Ang and Chua (1981, p.291) suggested that:

> managers of the acquired firms may lose jobs more rapidly than managers of firms that go bankrupt and successfully emerge from bankruptcy. If the distressed firm's management optimistically anticipate this outcome, management may prefer bankruptcy to merger.

Pastena and Ruland also hypothesized (in line with classical economic theory), that when a distressed firm is controlled by equity shareholders, rather than managers, their views are more likely to prevail. Furthermore, since shareholders of distressed firms should always prefer takeover (some value to stock) to failure (frequently no value to stock), the concentration of ownership amongst a few shareholders makes the company more amenable to takeover.

Company gearing

Ceteris paribus, Pastena and Ruland (ibid., p.293) hypothesized that the higher the leverage of a firm (the ratio of total debt to total assets), the more likely it is to fail than it is to be acquired. This is primarily because:

> If a low-leveraged firm acquired a high-leveraged firm, the leverage of the new firm will be higher than the original firm and the borrowing capacity will be reduced. While one might argue that the buyer can take debt into consideration in determining the offer price, it

seems more likely that potential buyers will
avoid the highly leveraged firms.

Corporate size

According to Pastena and Ruland, the rationale for
employing a variable (natural logarithm of deflated
sales revenue) which reflects corporate size is:

> Large firms and small firms differ in many
> respects and size empirically explains
> differences in many previous accounting studies
> ... size is an all-inclusive variable that can
> act as a surrogate for the many variables not
> included in the study. The direction of the
> possible association of size and the merger/
> bankruptcy choice is not clear (ibid., p.297).

Tax carryforwards

Under US tax laws, it is possible for an acquiring
firm to retain the tax loss carryforwards of an
acquired company, and thus set them off against
existing and future profits.
   Scott (1977), for example, concluded that tax loss
carryforwards is an additional feature which
encourages the acquisition of financially distressed
firms. Pastena and Ruland pointed out that tax
carryforwards (the ratio of loss carryforwards to
sales) has particular import in a bankruptcy/merger
setting; since 'they have value only if the firm
remains in business. If the firm terminates
operations the carryforwards are lost'. Hence, they
anticipated that carryforwards would be positively
correlated with the merger option.
   In fact, in their empirical model, this variable
proved to be an insignificant predictor. This
result is not too surprising. When consideration is
given to the fact that companies which eventually
fail are (if anything) more likely to have larger
tax carryforwards than those distressed firms which
are acquired, it seems reasonable to conclude that
it must be factors other than tax carryforwards
which make a financially distressed firm a more
attractive acquisition target (relative to one which
is allowed to fail).

Empirical findings

Having decided which variables to employ, Pastena and Ruland obtained samples of 42 failed and 68 distressed acquired manufacturing firms which were publicly traded in the US over the period 1970 to 1983. An initial sample of 531 acquired firms, on a research tape, were screened by Altman's (1968) failure prediction model. The model suggested that 83 (16 per cent) were failing (the sample was subsequently reduced to 68, due to missing data). This result is interesting in itself, since the proportion is similar to that (15 per cent) predicted as failing by Altman's model in the earlier Shrieves and Stevens study.

Using the econometric methodology of probit analysis, Pastena and Ruland reported that the overall classification accuracy of their model, in discriminating between failed and distressed acquired firms, amounted to 76 per cent (the classification errors within each group were not specified). Analysis of the variables revealed that ownership concentration, financial leverage, and size were all statistically significant predictors at the one per cent confidence level.

The signs on the variables indicated that distressed firms which were acquired had lower financial leverage, were larger, and had higher ownership concentration, than those which eventually failed.

As a consistency check, and using the same variable set, the authors also developed a multiple discriminant model. The resulting linear function correctly classified 87 per cent of the distressed acquired firms, and 57 per cent of those which failed (an overall classification accuracy of 75 per cent). A Lachenbruch jack-knife holdout prodedure was employed to test the out-of-sample predictive ability of the discriminant model. This procedure resulted in the correct classification of 81 per cent of the distressed takeover targets and 55 per cent of the failed companies (overall accuracy: 71 per cent). The authors concluded (ibid., p.300):

> The results show that size, leverage and ownership concentration dominated the explanatory model ... the results are consistent with the hypothesis that the self-interest of managers seems to be at least partly responsible

for the merger/bankruptcy choice.

Implications

Pastena and Ruland's study is an important development, since it is the first to demonstrate that, on the basis of only three explanatory variables, it is possible to discriminate between distressed firms which fail and those where a timely merger appears to serve as a viable alternative to liquidation. The classification accuracy of the model appeared impressive. It was able to accurately classify 71 per cent of the firms in the holdout sample. The probit model was also able to explain 53 per cent of the variation of the dichotomous dependent variable.

However, there still remain unanswered questions concerning the extent (if any) to which the decision-making process (motivation) of a company to acquire a distressed firm, irrespective of the 'managerial wishes' of the target firm, rather than permit it to fail, is reflected in the financial characteristics of the target firm. For example, two distressed firms with the same market shares, in the same industry, and with similar financial profiles, may nonetheless have different characteristics which make one a desirable acquisition target and the other not, and thus allowed to fail. These specific factors might include: (i) geographical/market location; (ii) asset structure/technology; (iii) distribution network; (iv) characteristics of customers; (v) corporate image; and (vi) research and development facilities. Factors such as these - and a myriad of others - are not necessarily reflected in a firm's financial ratios, but may nevertheless be attractive features to individual acquiring firms. Many would prove difficult, if not impossible, to accurately model.

To borrow from the merger literature, on the well known synergy argument of the "2+2=5" effect, those factors responsible for why: minus one (distressed acquisition), plus one (acquiring firm), equals two, may prove to be the most important, and elusive, explanatory variables pertaining to the liquidation/ merger alternative.

In this context, it is instructive to note that Altman (1971, p.122), in his book on corporate failure, provides an example of this latter point, with reference to the McDonnell-Douglas merger. He noted that this was an example of a situation 'where a merger quite probably headed off a financial disaster' (for Douglas). In 1966, Douglas sent out invitations to six large companies in respect of their expressed interest in aiding the beleaguered company. Two said 'no' immediately. McDonnell finally made a takeover offer: 'the McDonnell motivation was simple; sales diversification - not necessarily by product, but by customer'.

Insolvency buy-outs and industrial rescue

As was noted in Chapter 1, in relation to mergers, economic theory has traditionally concentrated on two broad classes of acquisition strategy/theory. The first, synergistic, derives from the combination of two enterprises - with gains emanating from increased market power, technical and related economies, the elimination of common functions, increased leverage potential, and risk reduction arising from less than perfectly correlated income streams (see e.g., Holl and Pickering, 1988; Lewellen, 1971).

The second is concerned with the replacement of incompetent management - often referred to as 'disciplinary' takeovers or the 'improved management hypothesis' (see e.g., Copeland and Weston, 1983; Jensen, 1986). As Shleifer, et. al., (1987, p.1) have noted, the purpose of disciplinary takeovers appears to be to correct non-value maximising practices of managers: 'such practices might include excessive growth and diversification, lavish consumption of perquisites, overpayment to employees and suppliers, or debt avoidance to secure a quiet life'.

This latter hypothesised rationale for takeovers, is very germane to the liquidation/merger alternative, since for a company whose main strengths lie in its managerial (turnaround) expertise, the prospects of 'picking up cheap' an ailing enterprise for turnaround purposes may prove to be particularly attractive (see Chapter 6).

Formed in 1983, the Gooding Group is a good example of a company which was instituted with the specific aim of acquiring failing firms for turnaround purposes. As Chambers (1985,p.20) has noted:

The Gooding Group is no asset stripping operation ... when it takes over a failing company the first step is to sack all the top managers humanely but swiftly: "you have to get it absolutely clear", asserts Gooding, "the people who are most vulnerable to takeover are top management. Middle management is generally looking for leadership, and when they get it they do a good job."

Referring to an alternative rationale for insolvency buy-outs, Copp (1983, p.3), of Stoy Haywood, stated: 'we often see purchases generate substantial profits, in a short time, from businesses acquired from insolvent situations, principally receivership'. Copp (ibid) concluded that:

Receivership will continue to provide good opportunities to purchasers of businesses, be they the former managers of the businesses or existing companies looking for expansion: ready made operations or production facilities can often be acquired from insolvent companies at a fraction of the cost which would be involved in developing these from scratch.

An alternative (but related) strategy to the acquisition of failing enterprises for turnaround is industrial rescue; an exercise, inter alia, performed by Investors in Industry (3i). According to Oates (1987, p.23), over a three year period, 3i's helped to rescue around 100 ailing firms, with a 90 per cent success rate. Again, the key to 3i's success appeared to be in the form of introducing new management blood:

It is far easier for someone coming in from outside to recognise that a company is heading for distress ... when we are called in, we immediately install a senior executive. He is employed to take whatever decision he considers appropriate, subject to the specific recovery plan agreed.

A recent example of a company which eventually called in the receiver, but which beforehand had attempted to both find an acquirer, and brought in turnaround expertise, is Sound Diffusion. As John (1988) noted:

> The company, which had been beset by major cancellations and delayed orders ... conceded defeat in its three-year battle for survival after its bankers withdrew support ... Chairman, Mr David Macdonald, who was brought in to try to turn the company around ... said there was not enough time to find a buyer for the business though the receiver would be under less pressure.

Management buy-outs

The 1980s, known as the decade of 'demergers', has witnessed a dramatic increase in management buy-outs. For example, in the UK, 13 management buyouts were recorded in 1977 (total value: £12m) rising to 261 in 1986, with a total value of £1,210m (Green, 1988; Robbie, 1988).

As Green (1988) has noted, the circumstances in which buy-outs arise are numerous; but one major factor, which accounts for a significant proportion, appears to emanate from the desire of parent companies to divest themselves of ailing subsidiaries - coupled with the fact that incumbent management perceive that they can rescue, or turnaround, these unwanted business units. In the last two years, however, management buy-outs have tended towards larger companies. As Robbie (op. cit.) has noted, at least 20 UK buy-outs in 1987 had been publicly announced for more than £25m, eight of which totalled in excess of £100m each. This trend appears to hinge on two major factors: more readily accessible funds in the city; and increasing competition between financial institutions.

Wright and Coyne (1985), in a study of 580 UK buy-outs between 1967 and 1983, discovered that a significant proportion were linked to failing (or failed) enterprises. In relation to management buy-outs in the private sector, Coyne and Wright found that there were five major circumstances where buyouts appeared to arise:

(i) receivership of an independent company. Here, a buy-out may represent the only method by which a company can continue in existence, and is often purchased in 'a reduced and reorganised form'. Five per cent of UK management buyouts fell into this category.

(ii) receivership of a parent company. In these circumstances a viable subsidiary is bought from a parent company, the remainder of which is liquidated. The subsidiary is thus sold to management as a going concern. Fourteen per cent of UK buy-outs in the Coyne and Wright sample were purchased on this basis.

(iii) divestment by parent company. Here, a viable parent company divests a subsidiary to management for strategic (non-insolvency) reasons. However, Coyne and Wright (ibid., p.149) did note that 'companies displaying post-buy-out cash flow problems are predominantly those divested from a parent still trading'. A large proportion (61 per cent) of UK management buy-outs fell into this category.

(iv) retirement or death of company owner. In these circumstances (21 per cent of buy-outs) the continuation of a company is secured by a 'succession' buy-out from the existing management team.

Unlike private buy-outs, and in contrast to the recent US 'junk bonding' phenomenon, management buy-outs of UK quoted companies were absent until the mid-1980s; since 1985, however, an increasing number of quoted buy-outs have been recorded (George, 1986; Wright, Coyne and Mills, 1987). A recent US study (Maupin, 1987), attempts to develop statistical models, based on accounting and market data, with the aim of predicting public corporations which go private via management buy-outs (see Chapter 5).

Corporate divestments

So far the discussion of the liquidation/merger alternative has focused on the acquisition of independent failing entities. However, an equally important area of acquisition strategy relates to the divestment by companies (usually conglomerates) of smaller business units, or 'lines of business'.

In a study of 436 divestments by large US corporations between 1974 and 1977, Ravenscraft and Scherer (1987) discovered that the overwhelming rationale for corporate divestments was in the form of unsatisfactory profit performance of specific business lines. In relation to 10,912 lines of business (business units) which were not divested, Ravenscraft and Scherer noted that the average return on assets (profitability) was around 14 per cent. However, of those business units which were divested, the average return on assets, over a seven year period before sell-off, was significantly lower, at 5 per cent.

More specifically, profitability declined significantly from seven per cent in year four before divestment, to a negative (loss-making) average of one per cent in the year before sell-off.

Ravenscraft and Scherer (ibid., p.190) concluded that:

> Poor and declining profitability, at the line of business or company level, or both, characteristically preceded sell-off for both acquired and original lines. Sell-off was, on average, a manifestation of financial distress ... our case studies revealed that substantial efficiency increases often occurred under the new organisations' structure, established following divestiture. Restructuring through sell-off was not a complete solution, as evidenced by the bankruptcies afflicting particularly distressed, highly leveraged, divestitures.

Discussion of the development of statistical models designed to predict when divestments will occur, is postponed until Chapter 5.

Summary

This chapter has reviewed the existing theory and (limited) empirical evidence pertaining to the bankruptcy/merger alternative. The early pronouncements of Dewey (1961), who suggested that most mergers were merely civilized alternatives to liquidation, have been subsequently disproved. The later empirical work of Shrieves and Stevens (1979), and Pastena and Ruland (1986), indicated that only about 15 per cent of US publicly traded manufacturing concerns were financially distressed when acquired.

However, the fact that most acquired firms are 'financially healthy', does not preclude bankruptcy avoidance acting as an important and significant motive for some mergers - a point not lost under US antitrust laws, where the Supreme Court may permit an otherwise unlawful merger to proceed, if it can be shown that the acquired firm would otherwise fail.

Furthermore, recent US empirical work by Ravenscraft and Scherer (1987) revealed that divested lines of business (business units) were, on average, loss-making (financially distressed) in the year before acquisition.

Chapters 3 and 4 provide new evidence on the liquidation/merger alternative in a UK setting. As well as replicating the Pastena and Ruland model, new models are presented which attempt to extend previous knowledge, by including a wider range of explanatory variables, and by analysing different corporate outcomes simultaneously.

3 The new study: research design, methodology and data

Introduction

This chapter outlines the methodology, data and variables employed in developing models aimed at discriminating between three corporate outcomes: liquidated firms, distressed acquired firms, and a control sample of non-failed ('healthy') firms. It also describes how the companies were selected into these groups, the variable selection procedures, together with a univariate analysis of the predictors; and provides a description of the sophisticated econometric methodology employed to estimate the various models.

The study is based on 383 UK quoted industrial companies, drawn from the period 1972 to 1979; comprising 47 failed companies, 40 randomly sampled non-failed (control) firms, and 296 acquired companies.

Chapter 4 presents the detailed multivariate (predictive) models which are based on these data.

Empirical aims

The primary aims of the study are:
(a) to collect sufficient data for UK quoted industrial companies to replicate the Pastena and Ruland US models of the bankruptcy/merger

alternative;

(b) to extend the limited variable set employed by Pastena and Ruland, to include a richer set of predictors suggested as appropriate by merger and corporate failure theory.

(c) to develop models specifically designed to discriminate simultaneously between corporate failure, distressed acquisition and continuing solvency (non-failed).

The Pastena and Ruland model, by limiting the outcomes to just two (failure and distressed acquisition) is excluding the possibility of the non-failed outcome, and it is thus effectively assigning a probability of zero to it. Hence, the development of multi-outcome models appears to be a logical extension of existing research, since such models would, if effective, allow the analyst, in evaluating a specific company, to assign a probability to this third outcome (rather than having to first evaluate a company with a failure prediction model, and then subsequently screen it with a merger/failure model).

Sampling procedure and data collection

All the company-specific data used in the study was obtained from the Extel Company Card Service, located at the University of Liverpool. The Extel Service, which covers all UK quoted companies, was originally installed at Liverpool University in 1972 and discontinued in 1979. Hence the data gathered for the study covers an eight year period, from 1972 to 1979.

The Extel Service annually updates the cards of each company, as new information is published. Normally, when a company is taken-over, fails, or loses its identity for some other reason, it is removed from the Extel system. Fortunately, this process was not followed at Liverpool, and thus, inter alia, companies which failed, or were taken-over, over the period 1972 to 1979, were not removed from the database.

Because previous corporate failure studies (Taffler, 1984) suggest that property, banking, investment and insurance companies exhibit significantly different financial characteristics from manufacturing and other industrial firms, they were excluded from the analysis. Extel company cards report the date of the first public announcement of failure (receiver appointed, court/creditor's winding-up) and takeover ('talks', takeover bid/agreed bid). In the study, only those firms whose last accounts were published before these first public announcements, were included in the estimation samples; since data after these announcements would have no predictive content. Different sampling procedures were used for each group of companies.

The failed sample

As in previous UK studies, failure is denoted by a company entering into receivership, a creditor's winding-up, or a compulsory winding-up by court order. An initial list of 81 quoted industrial companies, which failed between 1972 and 1979, was identified using information contained in the annually published Stock Exchange Official Year Book. A search was then made of the population of Extel cards and information on 47 failed companies was obtained. This initial sample was subsequently reduced to 40, due to public announcement after last accounts published and/or missing data - primarily the number of employees' and/or directors' shareholdings.

Data was collected from the last published accounts before the first public announcement of failure, and the previous year's accounts.

The non-failed sample

This sample was randomly selected from the Extel database. Because the Extel Company Card Service is annually updated, the data for these firms was obtained from 1978/79 accounts, and the previous year's accounts.

Most of the previous researchers who have developed failure prediction models have restricted their non-failed control samples to 'sound' or 'healthy' companies (see Altman, 1984; Taffler, 1984, for a review of these models). For example, the private failure prediction models developed by Tisshaw (1976) and by Taffler (1984) both excluded firms appearing less than 'healthy' from their non-failed samples. Hence a problem common to the 'traditional' two-group corporate failure analysis is that there appears to be a 'grey area' (e.g., loss-making firms) where the classification of firms as failed or non-failed is indeterminate.

This sampling methodology (screening) may be considered to be a particular empirical weakness, since it might be perceived as being more helpful to the user to correctly classify 'grey area' companies, rather than firms which more obviously fall into two discrete samples. This point is returned to in Chapter 6, but at this stage it is worth noting that the non-failed control sample employed in the study was randomly selected, and should thus be representative of the population of all quoted companies from which it was drawn; rather than from a potentially biased sub-set of 'healthy' (high performing) firms.

The distressed acquired sample

Because companies which are acquired (even if acutely distressed) do not formally fail, selecting a consistent sample of taken-over firms, which reveal signs of serious financial distress, presents a major problem.

An initial sample of 296 industrial quoted companies which were taken-over (at least 50 per cent of share capital acquired), over the period 1972 to 1979, was located following a systematic search of the Extel database. In contrast to Pastena and Ruland, a computerised database was not available to screen the companies in the initial sample. This would have facilitated the use of a Z-score model to 'predict' potential 'failure' candidates.

Instead, three criteria, suggested as appropriate by previous corporate failure studies, were employed to select the distressed acquired firms.

(i) Negative working capital   A company has negative working capital when its current liabilities exceed its current assets; or (equivalently), where its current ratio, of current assets to current liabilities, is less than one.

Newbould (1970, p. 157), in his book on business finance, stated: 'the current ratio and the liquidity ratio are indicators of the short-term survival of the company. The current ratio is usually taken to have a minimum of 1.5:1.'

Altman (1970, p.1170) in an early corporate failure study, also remarked that:

technical insolvency results when a firm is

unable to meet its cash obligations, and this can be measured by liquidity ratios such as working capital/total assets ratio ... We define technical insolvency as negative working capital/total assets.

Furthermore, Storey, et. al., (1987, p.178), in their recent study of small firm corporate failure, noted that:

Solvency of a company is critical to its survival and, although long-term insolvency is equivalent to company failure, it is short-term insolvency which precipitates the event ... short-term insolvency is defined as an excess of current liabilities over current assets.

Indeed, a review of US and UK failure prediction models developed since 1968 (see Altman, 1983; Taffler, 1984), reveals that the vast majority include, as a key explanatory variable, a measure of short-term insolvency (current ratio, or working capital/total assets ratio).

Furthermore, Mutchler (1984), who conducted structured interviews with sixteen auditing partners from the 'big eight' accounting firms, discovered that they considered that the current ratio, and the working capital to total assets ratio, were key factors influencing their decision whether or not to issue a going concern qualification (i.e., where the auditor has doubts about the continuing viability of a company).

Hence the accounts of the 296 acquired firms were examined and 23 (7.8 per cent) were found to have reported negative working capital in their last published accounts prior to the first public announcement of takeover. This sub-sample was subsequently reduced to 17, due to missing data observations.

(ii) Going concern qualifications   As Taffler and Tseung (1984) have noted, a company has its accounts qualified by an auditor: 'only on the basis that it might not continue in operational existence for the foreseeable future.' For example, the qualification is often given where a firm would otherwise fail, but for the continuing support of its bank (Lee, 1986).

A careful examination of the auditors' reports for the 296 acquired firms revealed that four (1.4 per cent) had their last accounts before acquisition qualified on the going concern basis. This sub-sample was subsequently reduced to two, due to missing data.

In relation to the going concern qualification as a basis for sampling distressed acquired firms, it is interesting to note that a recent empirical study by the author (Peel, 1989) concluded that failing firms issued with a going concern qualification were significantly more financially distressed than failing ones whose last accounts were not qualified on this basis.

(iii) <u>Loss-making firms</u>   As noted in Chapter 2, Boyle (1970), in a study which attempted to ascertain how many US acquired firms were at 'death's-door', and how many had been acquired as 'a response to actual or impending bankruptcy', used as his proxy for 'death's-door' the fact that a company had been losing money in the year before acquisition.

In addition, most previous failure prediction studies (Taffler, 1984) indicate that ratios reflecting profitability characteristics are key variables in determining a company's Z-score. For example, El Hennawy and Morris (1983, p.220) concluded that 'overall it is fairly clear that the major warning signal (of impending failure) appears to be low profitability'.

Hence, the last accounts of the 296 acquired firms were examined and 23 (7.8 per cent) were found to be loss-making (i.e., reported negative net profit before tax). This sub-sample was subsequently reduced to 20 due to missing data. Furthermore, in recognition of the fact that, due to turnarounds, loss-making firms do not necessarily continue on the downward slope to failure (see Slatter, 1984), the sub-sample of 20 distressed acquired firms was subsequently reduced to 13, by excluding those firms with a current ratio in excess of 1.2. This cut-off point was not chosen arbitrarily. Rather, it was selected with reference to the mean current ratio (1.1) of the failing firms employed in this study; and the mean ratio (1.3) of a sample of failed companies used by the pioneer of failure prediction models (Altman, 1968).

For these reasons, the initial sub-sample of 51

distressed acquired firms (17.2 per cent of all acquired firms), was subsequently reduced to 32. Of these, 19 had negative working capital (six of which were also making losses), and two had their last accounts qualified on the going concern basis. The remaining 13, based on their last accounts, were all loss-making, with a current ratio between 1 and 1.2.

No attempt was made to match the companies in each group by financial year end, size, or industry. Although some previous studies have indicated that ratios are not stable across wide industrial groupings (e.g., Taffler, 1984), others (e.g., Bank of England Model, 1982; Peel, et.al., 1986; Peel, 1987) have reported that pooling firms across industrial sectors does not appear to significantly impair the predictive ability of failure models. In any event, a number of studies have suggested that the appropriate criteria to be used for matching purposes are not obvious (e.g., Ohlson, 1980; Altman, 1983). A superior methodology would appear to be to use variables as predictors, rather than to use them for matching purposes. Hence in the study, company size and industry classification are employed as potential explanatory variables.

Estimation techniques

Most previous studies, whether attempting to predict corporate failure or mergers, have tended to use the statistical technique known as multiple discriminant analysis (see e.g., Altman, 1984; Taffler, 1984). Discriminant analysis (MDA) will classify a company into one, two, or more, groups (e.g., failed/non-failed) using vectors of predictors (Lachenbruck, 1975; Maddala, 1983).

In most applications, the derived discriminant function is a linear combination of the independent (explanatory) variables which most efficiently separate the two (or more) group centroids, represented by a binary or trichotomous dependent variable (e.g., dependent variables: failed/non-failed: 0,1; failed/non-failed/distressed acquis-ition: 1,2,3). For computational ease, MDA is employed to asses the predictive power of the various models in holdout samples (i.e., their discriminating ability on companies not used to estimate the models).

However, MDA presents a number of difficulties in interpreting associations between the dependent and independent variables (Hanushek, 1977); and hence logit analysis is used for this purpose, a technique which indicates changes in the probability of corporate outcomes, relative to changes in explanatory variables.

Logit/multilogit analysis

In recent years, logit/probit linear probability maximum likelihood estimators have become more popular in failure/merger prediction studies (e.g., Ohlson, 1980; Zavgren, 1985; Palepu, 1986; Storey, et. al., 1987). This is largely as a result of some well known statistical problems connected with MDA (Lo, 1986). The problems associated with MDA are:
(a) MDA requires that the independent variables are normally distributed and that the separate samples, from which the estimates are derived, have equal variance-covariance matrices; conditions which have been rarely met in previous studies.
(b) As Zavgren (1985, p.20) has observed, the linear combination of variables 'unique to a particular discriminant function, renders the importance of the individual coefficients impossible to assess.'

The use of conditional logit analysis avoids these problems because: no assumptions have to be made regarding the distribution of the independent variables; the coefficients derived from the logit/probit models estimate representative effects of population (asymptotic) parameters on the outcomes in the population; and asymptotic (large sample) theory is employed to test the statistical significance of the independent variables (t-values).

The explanatory power of the logit models is indicated by the McFadden's (1973) R^2. This is similar to the more familiar R^2 derived from least-squares regression estimates; in that it equals unity for a perfect fit and zero for no fit.

In models where the dependent variable is qualitative, a number of assumptions pertaining to the least-squares estimator are violated. Furthermore, the estimated (predicted) values of the dependent variable may lie outside the zero to unity range. These problems are surmounted by condensing the predicted probabilities within this range; by using either the linear logistic function, or the cumulative normal function (probit model).

In the study, logit and multilogit analysis (Maddala, 1983), the generalisation of logit analysis, are employed as estimators. This is because logit is computationally simpler than probit, which necessitates the use of non-linear estimating techniques. In any event, in terms of significance levels and explanatory power, the reported models of both estimators were almost identical. This in not too surprising, given they are directly related mathematically (see Aldrich and Nelson, 1984).

The Shazam (1982) statistical package was used to develop the dichotomous logit models, and Questat (1984) for the trichotomous multilogit models.

Explanatory variables

In total, 37 firm-specific financial data items were collected for each company (as shown in Appendix 1). In addition, eight non-financial (or qualitative) variables were also collected. From this data 74 financial ratios were computed for each company (see Appendix 2).

All the variables were derived from the last published accounts before first public announcement of failure/acquisition, and the previous year's accounts.

Variable selection

The variables were selected with reference to previous theoretical and applied corporate failure/ turnaround/merger studies (see e.g., Palepu, 1987; Belkaoui, 1978; Taffler, 1984).

The first seven variables are modelled on the predictors employed by Pastena and Ruland in their US study of the bankruptcy/merger alternative. The rationale for these predictors was outlined more fully in Chapter 2. The variables fall under the following categories:

1. Size   Two measures of company size are employed; that is, the natural logarithm of total assets, deflated by the Gross Domestic Product price index (SIZE); and the natural logarithm of sales, deflated by the Retail Price Index (SIZE1).

2. Gearing   This is a measure (TLTA) of company leverage; that is, the ratio of total liabilities (current liabilities plus long term debt) to total assets (current assets plus tangible fixed assets).

3. Ownership concentration   This is a binary variable (DSSH) for substantial shareholders; that is, where unity is used to denote that at least ten per cent of a company's ordinary shares are held by at least one individual or institution (zero, otherwise).

Because (in 1976) the mandatory reporting requirement for quoted companies in respect of substantial shareholdings was changed from ten to five per cent, substantial shareholdings were defined on the pre 1976 (10 per cent) basis; to ensure consistency across the inter-temporal samples.

4. Substantial shareholdings   This is an alternative (continuous) variable to DSSH. It comprises the number of ordinary shares held by substantial shareholders (ten per cent, or above), divided by the number of issued ordinary shares of the company (SSHN). It represents the proportion of a company's equity held by individual (substantial) shareholders; and is thus used as a proxy for ownership/control effects on directors' behaviour.

5. Directors' shareholdings   This variable is a proxy for directors' 'equity commitment' to their firm. It is measured as the proportion of ordinary shares held by directors (in aggregate), in the issued ordinary share capital of their company (DSNS).

The rationale for this variable is that, ceteris paribus, as insiders, the more failure prone directors perceive their company to be, the lower may be their equity commitment to it; in order to avoid personal capital losses (see Peel, 1985; Peel, et. al., 1986).

6. Directors' financial commitment   This variable is an alternative to DSNS, and is measured as the ratio of the aggregate market value of directors' ordinary shares in their company, to the aggregate value of their directors' remuneration (MVDR), in the year prior to acquisition/failure. Market value of directors' shareholdings is calculated by multiplying the mid-point of the highest and lowest share price of the company by the aggregate number of ordinary shares held by directors.

The motivation for this variable is that where directors (as 'insiders') consider that the probability of their company failing is high -

relative to takeover, where share prices usually rise significantly - they may attempt to lower the level of their shareholdings and/or increase the level of their current (risk free) directors' emoluments. Following this hypothesis, a comparatively high ratio is expected to be associated with the merger alternative, relative to corporate failure.

7. Tax carryforwards It was noted in Chapter 2 that under US law, tax loss carryforwards of acquisition targets may be utilised by acquiring firms. Further, Pastena and Ruland argued that carryforwards may be a significant factor in explaining the liquidation/merger alternative (although their empirical results failed to support this contention).

Under UK law, the benefits of carryforwards are less obvious. As Allan and Hodgkinson (1986, p.118) have commented:

> It is essential to realise that the target's losses cannot be offset against profits in the acquiring company or another member in the same group ... they can only be offset against the target's own post-acquisition taxable trading profits. These limitations on the use of trading losses indicate that their value should be discounted by a buyer to reflect their uncertainty.

In Chapter 2 it was argued, in contrast to Pastena and Ruland, that it was difficult to understand the rationale for this variable in a liquidation/merger context; since companies which fail should, if anything, have larger tax carryforwards and should thus, ceteris paribus, be expected to make more attractive acquisition targets.

Nevertheless, and despite the different legal regime, variables were collected to proxy potential tax carryforwards. These included deflated net profits (losses), in the year before acquisition/failure (DNP); and deflated accumulated earnings (losses) before interest and tax, in the two accounting periods before failure/acquisition (DAE).

In any event, none of these variables was able to discriminate significantly between UK failing and

50

distressed acquired firms, on either a univariate or multivariate basis. Furthermore, the mean values of these proxy tax carryforward variables, did not differ significantly between the failed firms and the distressed acquisition targets.

In a UK setting, therefore, there is no evidence to suggest that tax carryforwards are important factors in explaining the liquidation/merger alternative.

8. Liquidity/short-term solvency As noted earlier, the liquidity position of a firm is thought to be a key factor in explaining corporate failure; both by auditors and corporate failure model builders. In this study a number of standard ratios are employed to reflect a company's liquidity position. These are: working capital to total assets (WCTA); the current ratio, i.e., current assets to current liabilities (CACL); and current assets to total liabilities (CATL).

9. Leverage/long-term solvency When a company's liabilities exceed its assets it is said to be technically insolvent; that is, whether or not it enters into formal liquidation proceedings. Hence, the higher is company gearing, the higher is the perceived probability of corporate failure.

Not surprisingly, previous failure prediction studies (Altman, 1983; Taffler, 1984) have found leverage ratios to be key variables in failure prediction models. In addition to the gearing ratio (TLTA), the ratio of current liabilities to total assets (CLTA) was computed as an alternative leverage measure.

10. Profitability/managerial efficiency Ultimately, if a company continues to sustain losses, it will eventually fail. Hence variables measuring profitability (proxies for managerial efficiency), are consistently included as (significant) predictors in corporate failure models (Dambolena, 1983). Inter alia, the following profitability variables were computed: net profit before tax (NPBT) to sales (profit margin, NPS); NPBT to total assets (return on assets, NPTA); NPBT to current liabilities (NPCL); deflated earnings per share in the year before acquisition/failure (EPSD); deflated earnings per share in the previous year (EPSD1); and the change in deflated earnings per share between these two years (CEPS).

11. Activity   Two standard accounting ratios were computed in an attempt to proxy how efficiently companies utilise their asset-base to generate revenues. These were the ratio of sales to fixed assets (SFA); and sales to total assets (STA). In both cases, relatively low ratios are expected to be associated with the liquidation alternative.

12. Liabilities position   Variables were calculated in an attempt to proxy the capability of a firm to service its long and short term debt from generated revenues. The variables computed included: the ratio of sales to total liabilities (STL); funds flow to total liabilities (FFTL); and funds flow to current liabilities (FFCL). In all cases, relatively high ratios are expected to be associated with the merger alternative.

13. Gort's disturbance theory   As propounded by Gort (1969), the economic disturbance theory suggests that mergers should be more frequent when stock market valuations are showing rapid changes. The rationale is that since rapid movements in share prices, upward or downward, amount to a temporary economic disequilibrium, opportunities to gain from takeovers are then relatively high.

Following the methodology of Hughes, Mueller and Singh (1984), a number of variables were modelled with reference to Gort's hypothesis (PERA; PERA1; CPER; CHLPE; CHLPE1; CCHCPE). These are all based on changes between annual lowest and highest company price-earnings (PE) ratios, and are more fully described in Appendix 1.

14. Timeliness of reporting accounts   This variable is the time lag in lunar months (no. of days/28) between a company's financial year end and the date it published its annual accounts (as indicated in Extel cards).

The timeliness with which firms publish their annual accounts (LAG) has been found to be a significant predictor of corporate failure for large private companies (Peel, 1987; Peel and Peel, 1987); for small private firms (Storey, et.al., 1987); and for quoted companies up to three years before failure (Peel, 1985; Peel and Peel, 1988; Peel, Peel and Pope, 1986). In all these studies, longer time lags were found to be positively correlated with corporate failure.

The rationale for this variable is that the lag in

reporting accounts, and changes in the lag, may vary in sympathy with the 'news content' of the accounts ('good' or 'bad' news); and might thus act as an 'early warning signal' of impending financial distress, which will be eventually revealed in the accounts (in that a lengthening reporting lag can be observed before the accounts are actually published).

It has also been noted (Ohlson, 1980) that at least part of the reporting lag of financially distressed firms may be involuntary, since the auditing process for firms in poor shape may be 'particularly problematical and time consuming'. This reasoning certainly appears to be in accord with the professional observations of some notable practitioners in this area. For example, Homan (1984, p.35), national director of Insolvency Services for Price Waterhouse UK, concluded that 'late accounting should give as much cause for concern as faulty accounting - it is often the first tell-tale sign of trouble'.

Furthermore, McMillan (1984, p.9), managing partner, Arthur Andersen and Co., commented:

> Lack of timeliness in preparing annual accounts can be a sign of a problem. If the accounts are going to show a deterioration of a company's position, management will frequently delay publication while they try to find a solution to its problems; or, in some cases, just postpone the day of reckoning.

Because the 1976 Companies Act imposed new penalties on public companies which delayed publication of their accounts in excess of six months, and because previously the only pressure to produce timely accounts was exerted by the market and/or creditors, Student's t-values were calculated for the mean lag values of both the failed and distressed acquired firms pre and post the 1976 Act. The results indicated that there were no significant differences (at the 5 per cent level) between the mean timeliness of accounts, for both samples, before and after the 1976 Act. It was thus considered statistically appropriate to use the lag variable in pooled samples, pre and post the 1976 Act.

15. Industrial classification A binary variable was constructed to broadly reflect industrial classification; where unity is used to denote a predominantly manufacturing concern (zero, otherwise). The purpose of this variable (IND) is to capture any significant effects, across the samples, which might be associated with industrial classification (as broadly defined).

16. Going concern qualifications This is another binary variable (AQGC), where unity is used to denote that a company has received an auditor's going concern qualification in its last accounts before failure/acquisition (zero, otherwise). Such a qualification is given only on the basis that a firm might not 'continue in operational existence in the foreseeable future.'

Some recent research (Peel, 1989), discussed more fully in Chapter 6, has shown that failing firms which receive going concern qualifications in their last accounts are significantly more financially distressed than failing ones whose last accounts are not qualified on this basis. Hence, it is anticipated that this variable will be positively correlated with corporate collapse.

An examination of the accounts of the firms used in the study revealed that none of the non-failed companies had received a qualification; 11 (28 per cent) of the failed firms had their last accounts qualified; and two (6 per cent) of the distressed acquired firms were similarly qualified.

17. Share price movements Using monthly share price data, in an attempt to assess market anticipation of corporate failure, El Hennawy and Morris (1983a, p.359) found that 'analysts perceive a firm's difficulties on average at least as early as five years before failure'. Since share price data should incorporate any information not contained in financial ratios, a number of simple share price variables were computed for each firm.

These are based on the highest and lowest quoted share prices (as reported in Extel cards) for each company in the year before failure/acquisition, and the preceding year. To control for general movements in the market as a whole, the Stock Exchange All Share Price Index high and low point values were matched in time with those for each company.

The main market variables employed in the study

are the proportionate change in the lowest (LSP) and highest (HSP) share prices, for each company, over the two accounting periods before failure/ acquisition. In addition, market adjusted values of these variables were computed by deducting from LSP and HSP, the proportionate change in the lowest (SELSP), and highest (SEHSP), Stock Exchange index points (respectively), matched in time with the lowest and highest share prices of each company.

This produced two new explanatory variables: the market adjusted proportional change in the highest (AHSP), and lowest (ALSP), share price of each company, over the two accounting periods before acquisition/failure.

18. Remuneration levels   As was noted in Chapter 2, Vance (1971) suggested that a significant proportion of large US acquisition targets were shedding labour in the years preceding takeover.   Peel and Pope (1984) also hypothesized that the employees (or perhaps more correctly the unions) of financially distressed firms may limit wage claims in an effort to secure corporate survival.   To test for these potential effects, the following variables were collected: the proportionate change in the work force (CNE), and the proportionate change in the average real wage of employees (REMC), over the two accounting periods before acquisition/failure.

Furthermore, in a liquidation/merger context, changes in the behaviour of directors' remuneration, and changes in the ratio of directors' to employees' remuneration, in the period preceding acquisition/ failure, may act as an 'early warning signal' of forthcoming corporate change.   For example, if directors perceive that failure is imminent, and there is little chance of rescue in the form of a takeover, they may actually increase the level of their real remuneration.   In contrast, if directors of financially distressed firms consider that there is a reasonable chance of corporate survival via takeover, then they might also consider that the probability of this outcome would be enhanced if they constrained their emoluments to acceptable levels.

Hence, the following additional explanatory variables were computed: the proportional change in directors' aggregate deflated remuneration (CDR), over the two accounting periods before failure/ acquisition; and the ratio of aggregate directors' to aggregate employees' remuneration, in the year

before failure/acquisition (DER), and the preceding
year (DER1); and changes in this ratio (CDER).

Univariate analysis

This section compares and contrasts the financial
characteristics of the samples of failed, distressed
acquired, and non-failed firms, on a univariate
basis; that is, it investigates how well the
previously described variables can discriminate
individually between the samples. As well as
providing important information on the average
profile of the companies in each sample, univariate
analysis may also indicate potentially important
predictors which should be included in the
multivariate models described in Chapter 4.
    All tables referred to in this section are set out
in the appendix to this chapter.

Summary statistics

Summary statistics were calculated for each sample
in respect of the 74 variables shown in Appendix 2.
A Student's t-test was then applied to test for any
significant differences between group means.
    As between the failed and distressed acquired
firms, only 13 (18 per cent) of the variable means
differed significantly. This compares with 46 (62
per cent), which differed significantly between the
failed and non-failed samples; and 39 (53 per cent),
between the non-failed and distressed acquired
samples (see Appendix 2 for full details). This
analysis indicates, as might be anticipated, that
failed and distressed acquired firms had more
similar financial/non-financial characteristics than
the other two sample pairings.
    Table 3.1 shows ten general financial variables
(from the 13), which differed significantly between
the failed and distressed acquired samples. It is
interesting to note that, relative to distressed
acquired firms, failing firms were, on average:
more liquid (CACL, WCTA, CATL); had lower ratios of
sales to total liabilities, and funds flow to total
liabilities (STL, FFTL); issued a higher proportion
of new equity (CNS) in the year before failure;
experienced a more severe market adjusted fall in
highest share price (AHSP); received significantly
more going concern qualifications (AQGC); and were
significantly less timely in reporting their annual

accounts (LAG).

Overall, the variables which do differ significantly indicate that failing firms were (not surprisingly) more acutely financially distressed than distressed ones which were acquired.

When the group means which differ significantly between the other sample pairings are compared, excepting CNS and AQGC, the signs on, and magnitude of, the variables indicate that failing firms were significantly more financially distressed than distressed acquired ones; which, in turn, were significantly more financially distressed than a random control group of non-failed firms.

It is particularly interesting to note that failing firms, on average, exhibited a considerably longer time lag (LAG) in reporting annual accounts (7.08 lunar months), relative to the distressed acquired firms (5.81); which, in turn, were significantly less timely than the non-failed firms (4.43). This is consistent with the preceding observations, and suggests that timely reporting of annual accounts is negatively correlated with acuteness of corporate financial distress.

Table 3.2 shows summary statistics for the key variables associated with the liquidation/merger alternative. In all, the means of 13 variables are reported, for each sample, which replicate (and supplement) the predictors which were indicated as theoretically appropriate by the Pastena and Ruland model. As between the failed and distressed acquired firms, only two variables differ significantly. The first, measuring gearing (TLTA), is consistent with the findings of Pastena and Ruland; in that failing firms were, on average, more highly geared than distressed acquired ones.

The second indicates that aggregate directors' emoluments (CDR) of financially distressed takeover targets declined, on average, by 16 per cent in the year before acquisition. This differs significantly from the six and five per cent increases, respectively, associated with the directors of failed and non-failed companies; there being no significant difference between the latter groups. It appears, therefore, that relative to the directors of failed and non-failed firms, the directors of distressed takeover targets, on average, cut their remuneration bill significantly over the two accounting periods before acquisition.

However, and perhaps more importantly, on average, there are no significant differences between the failed and distressed acquired firms in respect of the following characteristics: firm size (SIZE); board size (BS); number of employees (NE); change in number of employees (CNE); the ratio of directors' to employees' remuneration (DER, DER1); the proportion of ordinary shares held by directors (DSNS); the proportion of ordinary shares held by substantial shareholders (SSHN); the ratio of the market value of directors' shareholdings to their aggregate remuneration (MVDR); and proxy tax carryforward variables (DNP, DAE).

In the year before failure, on average, directors of failing firms had an equity stake in their firms equivalent to a multiple of 4.8 (years) their current salary level (MVDR); a ratio which did not differ significantly from that of distressed acquired and non-failed firms.

It is also interesting to note that the non-failed control firms were, on average, significantly larger (SIZE), had a larger number of directors (BS), and a larger workforce (NE), than both the failed and distressed acquired ones. Furthermore, relative to non-failed firms, the failed and the distressed acquired firms, on average, reduced their labour-forces significantly over the two accounting periods before acquisition/failure.

To summarise, in respect of the Pastena and Ruland liquidation/merger alternative variables, only gearing, and the change in directors' emoluments, differed significantly between samples. Not surprisingly, failing companies proved to be more highly geared than distressed acquisition targets.

Hence, the summary statistics reveal that the average financial characteristics of failing and distressed acquired firms are more similar than the other sample pairings. In general, where significant differences were apparent, they simply indicated that failing firms were more acutely financially distressed than distressed acquisition targets; which, in turn, were more financially distressed than a random control sample of non-failed firms.

Univariate logit models

Although the summary statistics in the preceding section revealed how the average characteristics (variables) of the samples differed, they did not indicate their potential usefulness as predictors between the samples. A second univariate method

which does serve this function is logit analysis.
Tables 3.3 and 3.4 report 60 logit models which
are based on general financial variables (Table
3.3), and the more specific variables associated
with the liquidation/merger alternative (Table 3.4).
Table 3.3 reveals that, as between the failed and
distressed acquired firms, only six of the 12
reported variables are individually significant
predictors. The signs on, and the significance
levels of, these variables indicate (individually)
that, relative to distressed acquired firms, failing
ones were more likely to have: displayed higher
liquidity levels (WCTA); received a going concern
qualification (AQGC); suffered a sharper decline in
market adjusted share price (AHSP); exhibited lower
ratios of sales and funds flow to liabilities (STL,
FFTL); and to have delayed publication of annual
reports for a longer period (LAG).
It is also interesting to note that industrial
classification (IND); return on assets (NPTA);
deflated earnings per share (EPSD); and price
earnings ratios (PERA, CPER), are not significant
predictors in a liquidation/merger context; a fact
also evidenced by the low explanatory power of these
models (as measured by R^2). In the other sample
pairings, the logit models based on these variables
exhibit higher explanatory power and significance
levels.
These results tend to mirror (and confirm) the
earlier analysis in Table 3.1, directed towards
differences between sample means. That is, that
fewer traditional financial variables are able to
discriminate between the liquidation/merger
alternative; and that those which can, indicate that
failing firms are more financially distressed than
distressed acquisition targets.
Table 3.4 reports eight logit models which are
based on liquidation/merger variables, suggested as
theoretically appropriate by Pastena and Ruland. In
relation to the failed and distressed acquired
samples, only gearing (TLTA) is a significant
predictor, and explains five per cent of the
variation between groups. The coefficient of this
variable, not surprisingly, indicates that relative
to distressed acquisition, higher leverage is
associated with corporate failure. There is no
evidence to suggest that the proportion of shares
held by directors (DSNS), or substantial
shareholders (SSHN, DSSH), are significant
predictors in a liquidation/merger setting.

59

Furthermore, corporate size (SIZE), tax carryforwards (DNP, DAE), and the ratio of the market value of directors' shareholdings to their remuneration (MVDR), are also insignificant predictors. In addition, with the exception of size, gearing and tax carryforwards, the remaining liquidation/merger variables are unable to discriminate between the other sample pairings.

Overall, and excepting gearing, the univariate logit models reported in Table 3.4 offer no evidence in support of Pastena and Ruland's findings for the liquidation/merger alternative in a US corporate setting. The limited number of variables which are able to discriminate significantly suggest that failing firms had simply been allowed to progress further on the downward slope to liquidation; that is, they were more acutely financially distressed than distressed acquisition targets.

Summary

The main purpose of this chapter has been to describe the research design, methodology, data and variables employed to construct UK empirical models of the liquidation/merger alternative. The sampling procedures indicated that about 17 per cent of UK quoted industrial firms, acquired in the 1970s, were acutely financially distressed in the year before acquisition. This is similar to the proportion (15 per cent) of acquisition targets found to be financially distressed in two earlier US studies.

It appears reasonable to conclude, therefore, that a significant proportion (although a minority) of acquisition targets in both the US and UK are linked with the liquidation/merger alternative; or at least to corporate acquisition strategy which is targeted at ailing enterprises.

A univariate analysis of the explanatory variables revealed that, in general, failing companies were more acutely financially distressed than distressed acquisition targets; which, in turn, were found to be significantly more financially distressed than a control sample of non-failed firms. Other than in respect of corporate gearing, no evidence was found to support Pastena and Ruland's results for the US corporate sector; that is, that distressed acquisition targets are significantly larger, and have higher directors' and ownership concentration ratios, than similar firms which are liquidated.

Finally, the univariate analysis revealed that, relative to both failed and non-failed firms, the directors of distressed acquisition targets were, on average, reducing their aggregate remuneration significantly in the year before acquisition.

Whether this action was taken to improve reported profitability figures, or to enhance the incumbent directors' prospects of employment in the new post acquisition combination, is open to speculation.

Table 3.1

General variables: summary statistics

	Means[a]			T-values[b]		
	F	DA	NF	FDA	FNF	DANF
WCTA	0.06	-0.05	0.28	**	**	**
CACL	1.11	0.94	1.92	**	**	**
CATL	0.98	0.82	1.61	**	**	**
STL	2.01	2.96	3.84	*	**	*
FFTL	0.01	0.11	0.38	*	**	**
CNS	1004	112	1579	*	NS	**
LAG	7.08	5.81	4.43	*	**	**
AQGC	0.28	0.06	0.00	*	**	NS
HSP	-0.34	-0.15	0.11	*	**	**
AHSP	-0.35	-0.19	-0.05	*	**	*

[a]   F = failed; DA = distressed acquisition; NF = non-failed.

[b]   T-values for mean differences: NS = not significant; *, ** = significant difference at 5% and 1% levels respectively.

Table 3.2

Key variables: summary statistics

	Means[a]			T-values[b]		
	F	DA	NF	FDA	FNF	DANF
DSNS	0.36	0.30	0.12	NS	NS	NS
SSHN	0.18	0.15	0.10	NS	NS	NS
TLTA	0.76	0.66	0.48	**	**	**
SIZE	9.49	8.94	10.43	NS	**	**
MVDR	4.77	3.54	4.47	NS	NS	NS
BS	6.05	5.78	7.60	NS	**	**
NE	114	101	547	NS	**	*
CNE	-0.03	-0.05	0.02	NS	**	**
CDR	0.06	-0.16	0.05	*	NS	**
DER	0.04	0.05	0.03	NS	NS	NS
DER1	0.04	0.04	0.03	NS	NS	NS
DNP	-0.58	-0.19	7.61	NS	**	**
DAE	0.01	0.003	0.46	NS	**	**

[a] F = failed; DA = distressed acquisition; NF = non-failed.

[b] T-values for mean differences; NS = not significant; *, ** = significant difference at 5% and 1% levels respectively.

Table 3.3

Univariate logit models: general

No.	Var.	F v.DA Coef.	R²	F v.NF Coef.	R²	DA v.NF Coef.	R²
1	LAG	-0.28*	.07	-1.18*	.32	-0.97*	.20
2	AQGC	-1.74*	.06	-17.50*	.15	-5.49	.03
3	IND	-0.15	.00	-0.41	.01	-0.25	.00
4	AHSP	2.11*	.06	5.64*	.24	2.39*	.06
5	STL	0.44*	.06	1.22*	.30	0.35*	.07
6	FFTL	2.69*	.05	35.70*	.75	7.19*	.24
7	WCTA	-3.92*	.08	6.92*	.22	11.51*	.42
8	NPTA	1.79	.01	65.64*	.68	20.45*	.34
9	CLTA	-1.81	.02	-8.36*	.29	-5.78*	.15
10	PERA	-0.20	.01	0.01	.01	0.04	.06
11	CPER	-0.003	.00	0.02	.04	0.03	.05
12	EPSD	0.01	.00	0.52*	.48	0.28*	.29

* Indicates t-value of coefficient significant at 5% level or better.

Table 3.4

Univariate logit models: specific

No.	Var.	F v. DA Coef.	R²	F v. NF Coef.	R²	DA v. NF Coef.	R²
1	DSNS	-1.16	.01	-1.99	.02	-1.24	.01
2	SSHN	-0.78	.00	-2.37	.03	-2.05	.02
3	DSSH	0.30	.00	-2.01	.00	-0.48	.01
4	TLTA	-3.22*	.05	-12.61*	.42	-7.66*	.21
5	SIZE	-0.33	.02	0.59*	.11	1.01*	.23
6	MVDR	-0.05	.01	-0.01	.00	0.03	.00
7	DNP	0.0002	.00	-	-	-	-
8	DAE	0.0003	.00	-	-	-	-

* Indicates t-value of coefficient significant at 5% level or better.

4 The liquidation/merger alternative: empirical results

Introduction

This chapter reports a number of multivariate models developed from the data, samples and variables described in Chapter 3. The models are estimated using both logit/multilogit and discriminant/multidiscriminant statistical techniques.

One reason for employing two different estimators is to test the robustness (and comparative performance) of the models. Another is that, for computational ease, the out-of-sample predictive power of the various models is reported for the MDA functions only. However, logit/multilogit within-sample classification results are reported - with the added advantage that logistic coefficients can be tested for their statistical significance from zero.

The empirical results are presented in the following sequential format. Firstly, 'traditional' models based on the failed and non-failed (control) samples are reported. Secondly, estimates for models derived from the distressed acquired and non-failed samples are presented. This is followed by the key empirical estimates which focus on the bankruptcy/merger alternative. Finally, the chapter concludes by reporting multi-outcome models, which analyse the three corporate events simultaneously.

All statistical tables referred to in the text are reported at the end of the chapter.

Interpretation of discriminant models

The explanatory variables were selected for inclusion in the discriminant functions on the basis of the commonly used Wilk's Lambda stepwise procedure, a statistical process available on the SPSS computer package (Norusis, 1985).

With this procedure each variable is selected for inclusion on the basis of it producing the smallest Wilk's Lambda. With reference to F-statistics, only variables which were individually significant contributors to the discriminant functions at a 0.1 per cent statistical level were included in the models.

It was noted in Chapter 3 that evaluating the contribution of individual variables to an MDA model's discriminating ability is a task fraught with difficulties. However, F-to-remove values of included variables are reported. As noted by Klecka (1980, p.51) these statistics show:

> the rank order of the unique discriminating power carried by each of the selected variables. The variable with the largest F-to-remove makes the greatest contribution to overall discrimination above and beyond the contribution already made by other variables. The variable with the second largest F-to-remove is the second most important, and so on.

A Wilk's Lambda statistic is also reported for each MDA model. This shows the amount of variation of the dependent variable which is not accounted for. Hence it is an 'inverse measure', where one minus the Wilk's Lambda is equivalent to the proportion of explained variation.

An associated F-statistic, together with its significance level is given for each model. In the two-group cases, this tests whether the group centroids (or means) are significantly different. For the three-group models, it tests whether they are significantly different from zero.

Fisherian linear discriminant coefficients are used for classification purposes. This technique classifies a firm into the group assigned the highest score (for both the two and three-group cases). It produces identical classification results as would be achieved with a Z-score criterion with a cut-off point of zero (Norusis, op. cit., p.92).

Following the methodology of Altman (1971, p.68), validation (holdout) samples were obtained by randomly selecting eight companies (at a time) from the original samples, re-estimating the models from these reduced samples, and then using the new coefficients to predict corporate outcomes in the holdout samples. This is a generic test of the predictive ability of the models, since it is merely equivalent to commencing the research with reduced samples (-8) and then locating additional companies to form holdout samples.

No attempt was made to interpret the causal relationship between the discriminant parameters and the various 'predicted' outcomes. Given the statistical assumptions underpinning MDA (that the samples are each representative of their underlying populations, are separately distributed multivariate normal, and have common dispersion matrices), it would be 'unsafe' to follow this course. It also 'renders the importance of the individual coefficient impossible to assess.' (Zavgren, 1985, p.20). However, it has been noted that a violation of these assumptions is not thought to affect the classification ability of MDA models (Klecka, 1980; Ohlson, 1980).

Logit and multilogit analysis appears to be the appropriate technique for interpreting relationships between the dependent and independent (explanatory) variables; particularly where some of the latter are binary in nature.

Interpretation of logit/multilogit models

The logit coefficients reported for each model are interpreted in much the same way as for standard least squares multivariate estimates. Variables were selected for inclusion in the models on the basis of their predictive ability in the MDA models, the univariate results reported in Chapter 3, and those suggested as appropriate by extant empirical/theoretical evidence.

The explanatory power of the logit models is evaluated by reference to the McFadden's (1973) R^2 -

which is similar to the more familiar R^2 derived from least squares estimates; in that it equals unity for a perfect fit and zero for no fit. Efron's (1978) R^2 is used to gauge the explanatory power of the multilogit models. There are no fewer than 16 different measures of 'goodness of fit' which may be used in this context (see Amemiya, 1981). Efron's R^2 is employed for its ease of interpretation, since it is roughly equivalent to, or an 'analogue' of, the R^2 used in the standard regression model. In this respect:

it does not suffer from the deficiency of the number of wrong prediction ... since it corresponds to the sum of the squared residuals in the standard regression models from which R^2 is derived (ibid., p.1504).

The logit coefficients are interpreted in the following manner: a positive coefficient on a variable indicates the larger is its magnitude the more probable is the corporate outcome represented by unity in the binary dependent variable. Conversely a negative coefficient indicates the larger the magnitude of the variable, the more probable is the corporate event represented by zero in the dependent variable.

With the multilogit models, separate coefficients are generated for only two of the three outcomes represented by the trichotomous dependent variable. It is unnecessary to generate coefficients for the third outcome (i.e., distressed acquisition), since the probability of this event is derived by subtracting the sum of the predicted probabilities for the first two outcomes from unity (see Maddala, 1983).

However, the coefficients generated for the first two outcomes (fail/non-fail) are individually evaluated against the third outcome (distressed acquisition). For example, a positive coeffecient on a variable under option 1 or 2 (failed and non-failed, respectively) indicates the larger the size of the variable, the more probable is that event relative to distressed acquisition. Similarly, a negative parameter under either of these options would suggest the larger the value of the variable, the less probable are these events relative to distressed acquisition.

So far as classification is concerned, the multilogit model generates three probabilities - one for each corporate event (which sum to unity). The outcome with the highest predicted probability, for each company, is the group into which the firm is classified.

With the logit models, classification is achieved by analysing the predicted probability for each company, which is bounded by zero and unity (the dependent variable). In common with previous logit studies, a 0.5 cut-off point is employed for classification purposes. For example, the closer the predicted probability is to one, for a firm denoted by unity in the dependent variable (e.g., non-failed), the more accurate is that prediction. Conversely, for a company represented by zero (e.g. failure), the closer is the predicted value to zero, the more accurate is that prediction.

As has already been noted, the tables containing the empirical results are shown in the appendix at the end of this chapter.

Traditional models

The aim of developing traditional models from failed and non-failed (control) firms is two-fold:
(i) to compare their discriminating ability with subsequent models based on the other sample pairings; and
(ii) to 'screen' the sample of distressed acquired firms to ascertain the proportion 'predicted' as failing; as an ex post consistency test of the a priori sampling criteria described in Chapter 3.

Table 4.1 reports the most efficient discriminant model. Using the previously described stepwise technique, seven variables entered the model. The Wilk's Lambda for the discriminant function (0.20) indicates that a linear combination of the variables explains 80 per cent of the observed variation between groups (F-statistic significant at 0.1 per cent level).

As indicated by the F-to-remove values, the gearing ratio (TLTA) makes the largest contribution to the model; followed respectively by: current liabilities to capital (CLCAP); funds flow to current liabilities (FFCL); asset-turnover (STA); a going concern qualification (AQGC); company size (SIZE1); and change in (market-adjusted) annual highest share price (AHSP).

Within-sample, Table 4.1 shows that the MDA model correctly classified 95 per cent of the failed and 97 per cent of the non-failed firms (an overall accuracy of 96 per cent).

When the model was re-estimated from reduced samples, and the new coefficients applied to the holdout samples, its accuracy remained robust - correctly classifying 87 per cent of the failed and 100 per cent of the non-failed firms in the holdout samples (an overall accuracy of 94 per cent).

The within-sample classification accuracy of the re-estimated models (in the two reduced samples) also remained robust, with an identical overall classification accuracy of 96 per cent on each discriminant run. These classification results are consistent with previous UK models developed from failed and non-failed samples (Taffler, 1984).

Table 4.2 reports two of the 'best fitting' logit models developed from these samples. Other than for the timeliness of annual accounts (LAG), which is bordering on statistical significance, the coefficients of the independent variables in both models are all significantly different from zero (at the 5 per cent level or better) and appear to have the correct a priori signs.

Hence the parameters of Model 1 suggest that, relative to failed firms, the probability of non-failure (continued solvency) is increased the larger is company size, and the larger is the ratio of sales to total liabilities; and the more probable is failure the longer is the reporting lag of annual accounts, and the higher is corporate gearing.

Overall, the explanatory power of the MDA and logit models, and the interpretation of the explanatory variables, is consistent with previous work bearing on the traditional solvent/non-solvent outcomes.

It is recalled that one of the reasons for developing traditional models was to predict the failed/non-failed outcomes in the sample of distressed acquired firms (as a consistency check of the sampling methodology described in Chapter 3).

Model 2, reported in Table 4.2, predicted no less than 30 (94 per cent) of the 32 distressed acquired firms as failing. These are technically Type II errors (predicting non-failed as failed), and indicate that the sampling procedures employed to select the distressed acquired firms appear to be justified on an ex post basis.

A final and novel test of how distinct the samples

of failed and distressed acquired companies are, is made by pooling the distressed acquired firms with the failed ones and developing a discriminant model based on this pooled sample and the non-failed firms.

Hence, the failed (n=40) and distressed acquired (n=32) firms were assigned a common value of zero in the MDA model. The non-failed firms (n=40) were assigned a value of unity. Table 4.3 reports the resulting discriminant model, employing the Wilk's Lambda variable stepwise procedure described previously. The linear combination of variables was able to explain a high proportion (66 per cent) of the variation between groups.

What is even more surprising, however, is the within-sample classification accuracy of the model. It correctly classified 40 (100 per cent) of the non-failed firms and 66 (92 per cent) of the pooled sample of 72 failed and distressed acquired ones (an overall accuracy of 95 per cent). Furthermore, of those six distressed companies misclassified as non-failed, four were actually failed, only two were distressed acquired ones.

The empirical analysis presented in this section appears to have vindicated the sampling methodology adopted in Chapter 3. Consistent with the univariate results presented in that chapter, it also indicates that distressed acquired firms appear to exhibit a number of financial characteristics similar to failed ones.

Distressed acquisition and solvency models

This section presents the empirical models derived from the non-failed (solvent) and distressed acquired samples. Table 4.4 shows the most efficient discriminant model, together with its classification accuracy, which includes eight explanatory variables.

The model's Wilk's Lambda (0.22) suggests that 78 per cent of the variation between groups is explained (F-statistic significant at 0.1 per cent level). Company size (SIZE) makes the largest contribution of the function, followed by net profit margin (NPS); fixed asset turnover (SFA); directors' shareholdings (DSNS); liquidity (CATL); sales to liabilities (STL);change in price-earnings ratio (CPERAT); and gearing (TLTA).

Table 4.4 shows that within-sample the MDA model

correctly classified all the non-failed firms (100 per cent), with 31 (97 per cent) of the distressed acquired firms also classified correctly.

The holdout results are perhaps even more surprising. The reduced-sample discriminant model predicted with 100 per cent accuracy (the within-sample classification accuracy of the two reduced-sample discriminant runs also remained robust, with an average overall classification accuracy of 97 per cent).

Because of this unusual (but by no means unique) holdout result (Altman, 1973), in that the errors are normally higher out-of-sample, two more (different) groups of (eight) firms were withheld from the estimation sample as validation samples. The classification accuracy proved to be identical to the earlier holdout results. Hence the MDA model's accuracy remained robust under alternative model specifications.

A number of logit models were developed with the purpose of interpreting the influence (effects) of the explanatory variables. The most efficient was based on only four independent variables and is reported in Table 4.5.

All the variables appear to have the correct a priori signs and all are significant at the 5 per cent level (or better). The parameters of the model suggest that, relative to non-failed (solvent) firms, the probability of becoming a distressed acquisition target increases: the smaller is company size (SIZE); the longer is the time lag in reporting annual accounts (LAG); the higher is corporate leverage (TLTA); and the lower is corporate 'activity' (SFA).

In other words (and not surprisingly), all the parameters indicate that distressed acquisition targets were significantly more financially distressed than a random sample of non-acquired/solvent firms.

The proportion of variation in the dependent variable explained by the logit model is reasonably high (76 per cent) for data of this kind (see e.g., Peel and Peel, 1988); a fact reflected by its within-sample classification accuracy. It correctly classified 38 (95 per cent) of the non-failed firms and 30 (93 per cent) of the distressed acquisition targets (an overall accuracy of 95 per cent).

Overall, the classification accuracy and explanatory power of the MDA and logit models compare favourably with traditional models, derived

73

from failed and non-failed samples, and display a similar degree of group separation.

Liquidation/merger alternative models

The discriminant and logit models derived from the previous sample pairings illustrated that it was possible to discriminate between the failed/non-failed, and the non-failed/distressed acquisition, corporate outcomes with a reasonably high degree of accuracy.

This section focuses on models aimed at differentiating between the two financially distressed corporate states; that is, between those distressed firms which fail, and those where a timely merger appears to serve as a viable alternative to corporate collapse.

Given that both corporate 'states' have a common attribute (financial distress), a priori it is anticipated that statistical models, based only on financial variables derived from these samples, will be less efficient than traditional ones based on the more discrete solvent/non-solvent outcomes (an expectation supported by the univariate results reported in Chapter 3).

Replicating Pastena and Ruland

Table 4.6 reports two multivariate logit models which contain a range of variables suggested as being theoretically appropriate by Pastena and Ruland (Chapter 2).

Model 1 replicates Pastena and Ruland's model; whereas Model 2 contains an additional variable proxying directors' 'financial commitment' (MVDR).

In both models, none of the variables are statistically significant predictors (at the 5 per cent level) between the two samples. Further, other than for corporate gearing (TLTA), the explanatory variables have opposite signs (negative) to those hypothesised, and subsequently empirically validated, in the Pastena and Ruland study.

Hence there is no evidence to support the contention that the merger alternative is associated with larger corporate size (SIZE); a higher ratio of the value of directors' share capital to their remuneration (MVDR); a higher shareholders' ownership concentration ratio (SSHN); and higher directors' equity (ownership) commitment (DSNS).

Indeed, consistent with the univariate results presented in Chapter 3, the multivariate models, if anything, offer evidence to the contrary. Further, tax carryforward proxies (DNP, DAE), and the binary directors' ownership concentration variable (DSSH), also proved to be insignificant predictors.

So far as leverage (TLTA) is concerned, the influence of this variable is consistent with that postulated by Pastena and Ruland, and is a priori logical; since more highly geared firms would be expected to be more failure prone.

Not surprisingly, therefore, most of the explanatory power of the two logit models (8 and 9 per cent, respectively) emanates from this variable. However, the within-sample classificatory power of the two logit models is relatively low (64 and 68 per cent, respectively).

Hence, no support is found from UK corporate data to support Pastena and Ruland's conclusion that the 'self-interest of managers', as exemplified by the divorce between ownership and control, is 'at least partly responsible for the bankruptcy/merger choice'.

Discriminant models

Given that the logit models which included variables specified as theoretically appropriate proved unsuccessful, discriminant models were developed from stepwise procedures which utilized the whole variable set.

Table 4.7 shows the three most efficient discriminant functions to emerge. In Model 2, the liquidity ratio (CACL), a sampling criterion on which the distressed acquired firms were sampled, is omitted from the variable set (with the working capital/total assets ratio also omitted from Model 3 for similar reasons).

The Wilk's Lambda for Model 1 (0.63), suggests that a linear combination of the 'best fitting' variables is able to explain 37 per cent of the variation between groups (significantly lower than for the traditional models, and the non-failed/distressed acquired ones).

Most of the explanatory variables which enter the discriminant function are based on measures of liquidity (CACL, CATL, WCTA) and gearing (TLTA, CLTA). Other significant predictors include the proportional change in directors' remuneration (CDR), and in market adjusted highest annual share price (AHSP); the ratio of directors' to employees' remuneration (DRER); sales to total liabilities (STL); and the timeliness of reporting annual accounts (LAG).

Table 4.8 reports the classification results for Models 1 and 2 (Model 3 performed at a similar level to the latter).

Model 1 achieved the highest overall classification accuracy, correctly identifying 82 and 81 per cent of the firms in the estimation and holdout samples respectively (compared to 76 and 71 per cent, respectively, for the Pastena and Ruland models reported in Chapter 2).

However, the ability of the models to differentiate between these samples is somewhat lower than for the 'traditional' models based on the other sample pairings.

Logit models

Employing multivariate logit estimates, this section analyses the significance (and interpretation) of the variables which entered the discriminant models.

As might be anticipated, including all the variables in one logit model gave rise to multicollinearity problems. Hence, Table 4.9 presents three logit models which illustrate various combinations of the 'best fitting' explanatory variables.

Model 3 proved to be the most efficient, both in terms of its explanatory power and its overall classification accuracy. A linear combination of the seven predictors is able to explain 42 per cent of the variation between groups; a fact also reflected in its overall classification accuracy (79 per cent). Table 4.10 shows that the classification errors are more heavily distributed amongst the distressed acquired firms.

The model's significant parameters indicate that, relative to distressed acquisition, corporate failure is more probable: when an auditor's going concern qualification has been issued (AQGC); the higher is corporate liquidity (CACL); and the higher is the proportional increase in directors' remuneration (CDR).

The coefficients of the other variables are not statistically significant at the usual 5 per cent level. However, consistent with the univariate analysis, the coefficients of these variables suggest that: larger company size (SIZE), higher gearing (TLTA), a sharper decline in annual highest share price (AHSP), a longer time lag in reporting annual accounts (LAG), and a higher proportion of directors'to employees' remuneration (DRER), are all associated with failure, relative to distressed acquisition.

Implications

The empirical results presented in this section illustrate that , for UK corporate data, there is no evidence to support Pastena and Ruland's US findings on the liquidation/merger alternative; that is, that large company size, high ownership concentration ratios, and a high proportion of directors' shareholdings, are associated with the merger alternative.

Most of the variables which are significant predictors indicate that financially distressed firms which eventually failed were simply more acutely distressed than those which were acquired.

Interesting new evidence, however, revealed that directors of firms approaching failure appeared to remunerate themselves at significantly higher levels than those in financially distressed firms which were acquired.

Not surprisingly, the explanatory power and classification accuracy of the multivariate logit and discriminant models proved to be significantly lower than for those based on the more discrete failed/solvent - and solvent/distressed acquisition - sample pairings.

Multi-group models

Recent attempts have been made by researchers to extend the traditional binary corporate modelling approach to analyse three (or more) corporate outcomes simultaneously (see e.g., Peel, 1989; Peel and Peel, 1987; 1988).

This appears to be a logical extension of previous work; since it provides an analyst with the opportunity of evaluating (simultaneously) the probability of a number of alternative corporate 'events', rather than being restricted to the more traditional binary corporate outcomes (e.g., solvent/non-solvent).

This section utilises the technique, employing multilogit/multidiscriminant analysis, to predict between continuing corporate solvency (non-failed), corporate insolvency (failure), and the acquisition of financially distressed firms (distressed acquisition).

Multidiscriminant models

Table 4.11 reports a multidiscriminant model which was derived by applying the previously described stepwise procedure to the whole variable set.

In order of contribution to its explanatory power, the eight independent variables entered the model in the following sequence: working capital to total assets (WCTA); company size (SIZE); gearing (TLTA, CLTA); net profit margin over current liabilities (NPCL); timeliness of reporting annual accounts (LAG); going concern qualification (AQGC); and change in annual quoted highest market adjusted share price (AHSP).

The model's Wilk's Lambda (0.23), suggests that a linear combination of these eight variables explains 77 per cent of the observed variation between the three groups.

Table 4.12 shows that the model was able to correctly classify 80 and 71 per cent of the firms in the estimation and holdout samples (respectively). This is an impressive performance, since there are no fewer than six types of potential model classification errors (compared to only two in traditional models).

As might be anticipated from the two group analysis, the majority of classification errors are distributed between the failed and distressed acquired firms.

Multilogit models

Table 4.13 reports the most efficient multilogit model to emerge from various alternative combinations of the explanatory variables. It has seven variables in common the MDA model, with AHSP entering the latter in preference to fixed asset turnover (SFA) which is included in the former.

The coefficient of determination of the model ($R^2 = 0.70$) is reasonably high for pooled data of this type (see Peel and Peel, 1988), with a number of variables reaching levels of statistical significance.

Consistent with the two-group analysis, the signs on these variables suggest that, relative to corporate failure, the probability of becoming a distressed acquisition target increases: the lower is corporate leverage (TLTA, CLTA), and working capital to total assets (WCTA); the higher is fixed asset turnover (SFA); and where no going concern qualification has been issued (AQGC).

Other than for the leverage variable (CLTA), the parameters for the non-failed (solvent) outcome are consistent with the two-group models.

For example, the probability of non-failure/distressed acquisition increases: the higher is working capital to total assets (WCTA); the lower is corporate gearing (TLTA); the larger is company size (SIZE); and the higher is the net profit coverage of current liabilities (NPCL).

However, the sign on CLTA (current liabilities to total assets) appears perverse (negative), since a higher value of this variable is normally associated with corporate collapse.

Taffler (1983, p. 286) reports a similar result for a traditional solvent/non-solvent model. This problem appears to stem from simultaneity problems between explanatory variables. More specifically, Aldrich and Nelson (1984, p.46) noted that in the multilogit case:

> the signs of the coefficients (in specific instances) are not sufficient to determine the direction of change of the corresponding probabilities, this necessitates increased care in interpreting the results of polytomous logit models.

Table 4.14 shows that the within-sample classification accuracy of the model (82 per cent) is marginally superior to that of the three-group MDA model (80 per cent).

Again, the vast majority of classification errors are distributed between the failed and distressed acquired firms, with only one non-failed (solvent) company misclassified.

Summary

This chapter has presented a range of discriminant and logit models aimed at investigating the determinants of the liquidation/merger alternative in a UK setting.

In general, the multivariate results are consistent with the univariate analysis outlined in Chapter 3. High predictive accuracy was obtained from models derived from the solvent/distressed acquired samples, indicating that these firms exhibit significantly different financial characteristics.

Perhaps more importantly, in contrast to the empirical findings of Pastena and Ruland for the US corporate sector, variables reflecting company size, share-ownership concentration (control), and directors' 'equity commitment', were not found to be significant predictors of the liquidation/merger alternative in a UK setting.

However, a number of other financial/non-financial explanatory variables were able to discriminate between these outcomes with a reasonably high degree of accuracy (higher than that obtained by Pastena and Ruland).

An interpretation of these variables indicated that companies which failed were more acutely financially distressed than distressed ones which were acquired; and appear to have simply been 'allowed' to progress further on the downward slope to corporate collapse. Hence they did not appear to present themselves as desirable acquisition targets (e.g., on synergistic grounds) even sometime prior to collapse when they were still going concerns.

Discovering the 'attractive' features associated with financially distressed acquisition targets, relative to those which are 'permitted' to fail, must therefore remain the subject of further research. The next chapter, however, does attempt to examine the extant literature pertaining to the perceived rationale for, and gains emanating from, mergers and acquisitions in general.

The chapter concluded by presenting new multi-group models, which appeared to be able to discriminate reasonably efficiently between the three groups on the basis of published financial/non-financial information.

Table 4.1

Discriminant model: failed and non-failed*

Variable	F-to-remove
TLTA	33.8
CLCAP	16.6
FFCL	14.1
STA	10.5
AQGC	10.3
SIZE1	7.7
AHSP	3.4

Classification

Within-sample			Holdout sample		
F	NF	Total	F	NF	Total
38	39	77	7	8	15
(95%)	(97%)	(96%)	(87%)	(100%)	(94%)

* Wilk's Lambda = 0.20; equivalent F-value = 32.8 (significant at 0.1% level).

Table 4.2

Logit models: failed and non-failed

	Model 1		Model 2	
Var.	Coeff.	t-value	Coeff.	t-value
SIZE1	0.71	2.25*	0.64	2.21*
LAG	-1.82	2.03*	-0.65	1.91
TLTA	-14.75	2.27*	-	-
WCTA	-	-	5.01	2.26*
STL	1.08	2.17*	-	-
CON.	-7.28	1.80	-3.53	1.03
R^2	0.82	-	0.60	-

* Indicates t-value of coefficient significant at
5% level or better.

Table 4.3

Discriminant model: NF v. FDA[ab]

Variable	F-to-remove
SIZE1	25.2
WCTA	21.2
TLTA	15.7
NPCL	12.4
CLTA	10.9

[a] NF v. FDA = 40 non-failed versus 72 grouped failed and distressed acquired firms.

[b] Wilk's Lambda = 0.34; equivalent F-value = 34.1 (significant at 0.1% level).

Table 4.4

Discriminant model: NF v. DA*

Variable	F-to-remove
SIZE	45.8
NPS	33.4
SFA	19.3
DSNS	13.9
CATL	8.6
STL	7.9
CPER	5.1
TLTA	4.3

Classification

Within-sample			Holdout sample		
NF	DA	Total	NF	DA	Total
40	31	71	8	8	16
(100%)	(97%)	(98%)	(100%)	(100%)	(100%)

* Wilk's Lambda = 0.22; equivalent F-value = 27.6
(significant at 0.1% level).

Table 4.5

Logit model: NF v. DA

Variable	Coefficient	t-value
SIZE	1.99	2.83*
LAG	-1.54	2.22*
TLTA	21.77	2.90*
SFA	0.47	2.41*
CON.	-0.89	0.16

McFadden's R^2 = 0.76

Classification

Non-failed	Distressed acquisition	Total
38	30	68
(95%)	(93%)	(94%)

* Indicates t-value of coefficient significant at
  5% level or better.

Table 4.6

Logit models: liquidation/merger variables

	Model 1		Model 2	
Var.	Coeff.	t-value	Coeff.	t-value
TLTA	-2.59	1.55	-3.38	1.91
SIZE	-0.35	1.36	-0.31	1.15
DSNS	-2.08	1.12	-1.93	0.91
SSHN	-1.49	1.10	-1.55	1.16
MVDR	–	–	-0.01	0.12
CON.	5.23	2.18*	5.49	2.16*
R^2	0.08	–	0.09	–

* Indicates t-value of coefficient significant at 5% level (n = 72; 40 failed and 32 distressed acquired firms).

Table 4.7

MDA models: failed and distressed acquisitions

Variables	Model 1 F-values[a]	Model 2 F-values[a]	Model 3 F-values[a]
CACL	22.2	-	-
WCTA	-	14.3	-
STL	-	3.2	-
CDR	5.8	5.3	5.5
DRER	6.1	1.2	2.9
TLTA	-	-	5.2
CATL	-	-	16.9
AQGC	7.9	8.7	5.7
AHSP	2.2	-	1.5
LAG	-	2.7	-
CLTA	2.7	-	-
WL[b]	0.60	0.63	0.63
F-VALUE[c]	7.1	6.1	6.3

[a] Indicates F-to-remove values.

[b] WL = Wilk's Lambda.

[c] F-values for differences between group centroids (all significant at 0.1% level).

Table 4.8

MDA classification accuracy: F v. DA*

Within-sample

Model 1			Model 2		
F	DA	Total	F	DA	Total
34	25	59	34	24	58
(85%)	(78%)	(82%)	(85%)	(75%)	(81%)

Holdout sample

Model 1			Model 2		
F	DA	Total	F	DA	Total
6	7	13	5	7	12
(75%)	(87%)	(81%)	(63%)	(87%)	(75%)

* F = failed samples; DA = distressed acquisition
   samples.

Table 4.9

Logit models: failed and distressed acquisitions

Var.	Model 1 Coeff.	Model 2 Coeff.	Model 3 Coeff.
AQGC	-2.67*	-2.35**	-2.64**
	(2.5)	(2.1)	(2.2)
LAG	-0.34**	-0.35**	-0.36***
	(2.0)	(2.0)	(1.8)
CACL	-5.32*	-5.91*	-6.68*
	(3.3)	(3.3)	(3.2)
CDR	-0.07*	-0.07**	-0.08**
	(2.4)	(2.3)	(2.3)
SIZE	-0.53	-0.42	-0.49
	(1.5)	(1.2)	(1.2)
AHSP	-	-	2.4***
			(1.8)
DRER	-14.5	-16.2	-20.8***
	(1.4)	(1.6)	(1.7)
TLTA	-	-3.98	-4.07
		(1.5)	(1.5)
CON.	13.4*	15.9*	18.3*
	(2.8)	(2.9)	(2.8)
R^2	0.36	0.39	0.42

*, **, *** Indicates t-value for coefficient (in parenthesis) is significant at 1%, 5% and 10% levels respectively.

Table 4.10

Logit model classification: F v. DA*

	Model 1			Model 2	
F	DA	Total	F	DA	Total
34	23	57	33	22	55
(85%)	(72%)	(79%)	(83%)	(69%)	(76%)

Model 3

F	DA	Total
34	23	57
(85%)	(72%)	(79%)

* F = failed sample; DA = distressed acquisition sample.

Table 4.11

Three group MDA model[a]

Variable	F-to-remove[b]
WCTA	24.2
SIZE	11.5
TLTA	9.2
CLTA	8.1
NPCL	7.5
LAG	4.9
AQGC	3.8
AHSP	3.5

[a] Samples = 40 failed; 40 non-failed; and 32 distressed acquired firms.

[b] Wilk's Lambda = 0.32; equivalent F-value = 34.1 (significant at 0.1% level).

Table 4.12

Three group MDA model: classification

Within-sample

Actual groups[a]   Predicted groups[b]

	F	NF	DA
F = 40	27*	3	10
	(67.5%)	(7.5%)	(25.0%)
NF = 40	1	39*	0
	(2.5%)	(97.5%)	(0.0%)
DA = 32	8	0	24*
	(25.0%)	(0.0%)	(75.0%)

Holdout sample

Actual groups[a]   Predicted groups[c]

	F	NF	DA
F = 8	5*	0	3
	(62.5%)	(0.0%)	(37.5%)
NF = 8	0	7*	1
	(0.0%)	(87.5%)	(12.5%)
DA = 8	3	0	5*
	(37.5%)	(0.0%)	(62.5%)

[a] F = failed firms; NF = non-failed firms; DA = distressed acquired firms.

[b] Overall three group accuracy = 80.4%.

[c] Overall three group accuracy = 70.8%.

* Indicates correct group predictions.

Table 4.13

Three group multilogit model

Variables[a]	Failed coefficients[b]	Non-failed coefficients[b]
WCTA	12.9* (3.7)	20.1* (2.6)
LAG	0.34 (1.8)	-0.96 (1.3)
TLTA	2.3 (0.6)	-26.1* (2.7)
SIZE	0.10 (0.3)	1.9* (2.5)
SFA	-0.17* (2.2)	0.23 (1.1)
CLTA	9.9* (2.1)	29.9* (2.6)
NPCL	1.6 (0.8)	13.2* (2.2)
AQGC	2.6* (2.1)	-0.78 (0.36)
CON.	-7.7 (1.6)	-46.1* (2.9)

Efron's R^2 = 0.70

[a] Dependent variable: 1 = failed; 2 = non-failed; 3 = distressed acquisition.

[b] Unnecessary to estimate coefficients for distressed acquisition alternative.

* Indicates t-value for coefficient (in parenthesis) is significant at 5% level or better.

Table 4.14

Multilogit model: classification

Actual groups[a]	Predicted groups[b]		
	F	NF	DA
F = 40	31*	2	7
	(77.5%)	(5.0%)	(17.5%)
NF = 40	1	39*	0
	(2.5%)	(97.5%)	(0.0%)
DA = 32	10	0	22*
	(31.2%)	(0.0%)	(68.8%)

[a] F = failed firms; NF = non-failed firms; DA = distressed acquired firms.

[b] Overall three group accuracy = 82.1%.

* Indicates correct group predictions.

5 Mergers, buy-outs and divestments: some extensions

Introduction

The aim of this chapter is to provide a summary of recent theoretical and empirical developments pertaining to the rationale for, and impact of, acquisitions, management buy-outs and corporate divestments.

No attempt is made to provide a comprehensive review of the copious extant literature (see e.g., Hughes, et. al., 1984; Hughes, 1987; Jensen and Ruback, 1983); rather key developments which bear on, and supplement, the work in preceding chapters are outlined.

It was noted in Chapter 2 that the literature on merger motivation is classified into two broad groupings. The neoclassical (shareholder wealth-maximising) approach hypothesises that managers will pursue mergers and acquisitions when such investments offer a positive (estimated) net present value - which may emanate from increased market power (e.g., price-setting), synergies, removal of incompetent management and from financial benefits (such as risk reduction arising from imperfectly correlated income streams).

The new managerial theories, however, argue that with the divorce between ownership and control, managers may seek to maximise their own self-interests; and where their own shareholdings are relatively low, they may not be congruent with those of shareholders (Jensen and Meckling, 1976). As Taffler and Holl (1988, p. 75) have noted:

> managers may be seeking to maximise their own self-interest in the form of power, salary and reduction in the risk of job loss subject to satisfactory profitability. Such aims may be achieved through size maximisation and takeover is the quickest method of growth.

However, the two theories are indirectly related; since it is hypothesized that if managers pursue their own (non-profit maximising) motives, other corporate managers, who are seeking to maximise returns, will exert a 'disciplinary' or 'reforming' effect on them - via the 'market for corporate control'(Manne, 1965).

Under this hypothesis, competition in the market for corporate control ensures that a potentially large supply of predators exists to penalise managers who are pursuing goals other than the maximisation of shareholder wealth - or who inefficiently manage corporate assets. Here, the threat of takeover should discipline incumbent management to improve efficiency; those who do not will be subsumed by predators.

Empirical research on these issues has broadly followed two paths:

(i) the collection of primary data, through questionnaires and structured interviews, from the participants in mergers; and

(ii) the collection of secondary financial and market data, pre and post merger, to assess relative gains and/or losses to shareholders, and the characteristics of acquirers and targets.

Although a number of researchers have reported conflicting evidence, an international review of 27 major empirical merger studies, spanning the period 1971 to 1985, by Hall and Norburn (1987, p. 23), concluded:

> (1) Returns to shareholders of acquiring firms are, at best, slight and tend to disappear rapidly, and, at worst, are significantly negative.

(2) Returns to shareholders of acquired firms are strongly positive.
(3) Gains and losses of victims and predators become a zero sum.
(4) In certain cases, a failed bid leads to improved stock market valuation.
(5) Acquisitions are unlikely to reduce risk.

Hence, international evidence on merger activity suggests that shareholder wealth-maximising theories are largely unsupported, in that no 'real' merger gains are apparent - and 'the impact for acquiring companies' shareholders is at best neutral'.

In another recent review of UK empirical evidence pertaining to mergers, Hughes (1987, p. 87) concluded that although some firms had grown 'spectacularly fast' by non-horizontal merger: 'the implications for market power of these changes are ambiguous and probably less important than their broader impact on the nature of resource allocation'. He also noted that takeover, or the threat of it, as a stock market disciplinary device, was constrained - except at the height of 'booms' - to 'middle-range' companies: 'the most favourable route is to grow bigger and seek more stable profits in the short run, than to go for higher medium term profitability'. From the prevailing evidence Hughes (ibid., p. 85) concluded:

The disciplinarians are bigger and faster growing, but not on average more profitable, and their shareholders gain little or even lose ... shareholders of acquired companies on the other hand make windfall gains ... if these gains are supposed to represent expected performance improvements then direct evidence on the latter suggests that the market gets it wrong and on average has been too optimistic. All this evidence seems at least as consistent with an inducement to empire building, by growth-minded managers, as much as discipline in the stockholders interests.

The remainder of this chapter focuses on a selection of recent studies which provide new evidence on these issues.

Managerial motivation for mergers

From the preceding analysis, it seems clear that the weight of existing empirical evidence fails to support a simple (or comprehensive) rationale for mergers in terms of a 'real gains' scenario for stockholders.

This has led to a realisation that 'management motives for making acquisitions differ and thus today's perception of success or failure must be a composite measure setting current satisfaction levels against the original motives' (Kitching, 1967).

Hence a number of studies have examined the perceived rationale of managers for undertaking mergers. In one of the earliest, Newbould (1970), after interviewing senior managers responsible for acquisitions in 38 UK companies in 1967/68, reported that none referred explicitly to the maximisation of shareholder wealth as a motivating factor. Of the reasons proffered, seven mergers (18 per cent) were explained as defensive or strategic, such as the desire to maintain or increase market share; an equal number were (surprisingly) explained in terms of the target company approaching the acquirer with the merger proposal; other prime motivating factors included 'growth by acquisition' (16 per cent) and acquisition as a response to 'increasingly difficult business conditions' (13 per cent).

Furthermore, Newbould noted that little analysis of target firms appeared to be undertaken by acquirers; what was appeared to be of a 'basic variety' - and for 15 of the 38 mergers (39 per cent) it took less than one month to complete.

In a more international context, a report by OECD (1974) listed twelve primary managerial motivating factors for making acquisitions: (1) to increase market power; (2) to build an empire; (3) to gain promotional profits; (4) to expand production without price reduction; (5) to acquire capacity at reduced prices; (6) to obtain real economies of scale; (7) to obtain monetary economies; (8) to rationalize production; (9) to use complementary resources; (10) to spread risk by diversification; (11) to avoid a firm's failure; and (12) to merge for tax advantages.

However, Boucher (1980), in a Federal Trade Commission study, categorised no less than 31 managerial motives for making acquisitions. Based on interviews with a large sample of respondents, the most important factors, in descending order (with scores in parenthesis), were as follows:

(i)   to take advantage of an undervalued company (18.2);
(ii)   to achieve growth more rapidly than by internal expansion (16.9);
(iii)   to meet demand for additional product services;
(iv)   avoiding risks associated with internal expansion or start-ups (16.9);
(v)   increasing earnings per share (14.2);
(vi)   reducing dependence on a single service or product (13.5);
(vii)   to acquire market share/position (11.6);
(viii)   to offset seasonal or cyclical fluctuations in present operations (10.5);
(ix)   to enhance the power and prestige of the current owners/ managers (10.2);
(x)   to increase the utilisation of existing plant/resources (9.3);
(xi)   to acquire managerial/technical personnel (8.9); and
(xii)   to open new markets for existing products/services (8.3).

In a recent study of 40 acquisitions made by major UK companies, Hunt and Lees (1987, p. 117) found no evidence to support the 'predator myth'; and in stark contrast to Newbould's earlier study:

Rather than a hasty, ill-conceived process, the researchers found the opposite: a long, well-considered period of observing the target, a carefully orchestrated period of negotiation, and, finally, a clearly communicated, if not documented, vision which is implemented through a pattern of empirically significant buyer behaviours.

Surprisingly, only 10 per cent of acquisitions in their sample were hostile; 45 per cent were 'completely amicable'; with a further 45 per cent 'friendly but partly hostile'. Hunt and Lees also investigated the myth of the 'predator stereotype'. They discovered that 'the popular image of the predator, flush with money, coldly and analytically targeting the innocent seller, is largely false.

For 30 per cent of the sample, the seller actually approached the buyer first'.

Furthermore, Hunt and Lees discovered that contrary to the 'sleuth-like' view of takeovers held by many specialists, 'most acquisitions are championed by the chairman who digests the information during the monitoring phase'. Further, most frequently, it is 'the chairman and one or two other senior executives who negotiate the whole deal from beginning to end'. Hunt and Lees (ibid., p. 117) also noted that:

> Most buyers are so quiet and underdramatic when they are stalking that 63 per cent of sellers did not know they were being watched. This is despite the fact that audits of the prey were carried out in all cases ... Some were superficial; others were textbook examples of audit precision ... in nearly all cases an audit of the people the buyer intended to buy were either considered impossible or, if possible, regarded as not very important.

In relation to the stated managerial reasons for mergers, Hunt and Lees (ibid., p. 117) noted that market share was the prime motivating factor: 'ROI or ESP are not the prime objectives, by far the most important reason was market share or new markets, or both, which motivated the chairman's search'.

The 'top ten' motivating factors, in descending order of importance, were: (1) for market share; (2) sending 'signals to the City'; (3) for technical capabilities; (4) on the chairman's 'insistence'; (5) for management capabilities; (6) to improve ROI; (7) for synergy/economies of scale; (8) defending markets; (9) for assets; (10) to 'retrieve face'.

Although managerial studies offer interesting new evidence pertaining to the perceived rationale for acquisitions, and to the merger process, other than in the OECD report, no explicit reference was made by managers to factors associated with the liquidation/merger alternative. However, that 18 and 30 per cent of acquisitions, respectively, in the Newbould and Hunt and Lees studies, were initially triggered by target firms, may be indicative (at least partly) of 'bankruptcy avoidance' being a 'hidden' motivating factor for these firms.

Mergers and acquisitions: determinants and effects

This section reports the results of some recent empirical research which has investigated the causes and effects of mergers and acquisitions. In particular, it focuses on the 'classical' versus 'managerial' theories as explanations for merger activity.

Actual, abandoned, hostile and friendly mergers

Actual and abandoned mergers   Using samples of 50 actual, 50 abandoned and 33 contested merger cases, pertaining to UK quoted companies over the period 1965 to 1975, Holl and Pickering (1988) examined the determinants and effects of actual, abandoned and contested mergers.

A large number of potential explanatory variables were collected in an attempt to reflect managerial, shareholder and 'financial status' characteristics. Their key empirical results were as follows:

(i) A greater performance difference existed between bidders and targets in successful mergers compared to those which were abandoned. Targets which were acquired exhibited an inferior performance level, relative to targets which had successfully resisted merger (and their bidders). Holl and Pickering (ibid., p. 15) concluded:

> the greater inherent strengths of targets in abandoned mergers (reflected particularly by their performance over the previous three years) seems to have been a prime reason why those mergers did not take place.

(ii) acquired companies appeared to be slower growing, less profitable and smaller than both their acquirers and firms which had successfully resisted takeover.

(iii) successful bidders exhibited higher measures of gearing, liquidity, retentions and faster growth; but, on average, did not produce higher returns to shareholders: 'it would appear that fast growth and financial strength are more important influences on bidding success than profit orientation'.

(iv) firms which were involved in unsuccessful merger bids subsequently performed at a superior level to participants involved in successful ones -

particularly in respect of 'financial strength' and shareholder returns.

Holl and Pickering (ibid) concluded that, overall, their empirical evidence:

> gives some grounds for continuing concern that the merger process rewards those whose emphasis is on 'managerial' objectives, and precludes those whose main failing is that they are not large enough. However, this latter position is not fully supported, since we show that companies which are taken-over do also tend to have inferior performances in other respects and that those bid-for companies which escape being acquired do have a stronger medium-term performance record.

Abandoned mergers and corporate control   Using samples of UK quoted companies, over the period 1977 to 1981, Taffler and Holl (1988) examined the performance characteristics of 129 acquired firms, 76 acquiring companies and 55 targets in abandoned mergers.

Company accounts data was analysed to test for any evidence of a 'disciplinary effect' exercised by the market for corporate control (utilising 'PAS-scores' derived from a Z-score model). In Taffler and Holl's view:

> this method provides an holistic measure of economic performance allowing inter-temporal and cross-section comparisons explicitly, and overcomes many of the problems associated with the conventional use of profitability ratios (ibid., p. 4).

Their main empirical findings were as follows:
(i)   no empirical evidence was found in support of the hypothesis that 'financially strong' firms acquire weaker ones: 'on the contrary, strong companies are taking over other strong companies'.
(ii)   in relation to abandoned mergers, the authors also discovered no evidence to suggest that 'the market for corporate control exercises discipline on underperforming companies.   The post bid financial performance of both bidding and target companies

showed no significant improvement'.

(iii) bidding companies in abandoned mergers appeared to be significantly 'weaker' than the companies they bid for: 'it seems that in the case of abandoned mergers inherently weak companies are attempting to takeover companies which are inherently stable'.

The Taffler and Holl study is an important addition to the extant literature, since it offers no support for the 'disciplinary hypothesis' of the market for corporate control - at least in a UK setting.

Hostile and friendly targets   Using probit and difference between means analysis, Shleifer, Vishny and Morck (1987) attempted to test the hypothesis that disciplinary takeovers are likely to be more 'hostile' than synergistic ('friendly') ones.

Their analysis was based on data derived from 454 publicly traded firms drawn from Fortune's 500 in 1980. Of these, 82 had been acquired or were the subject of a management buy-out. An acquisition was classified as hostile if the initial bid was rejected by the target's board, or if there was 'active management resistance to the bid, escape to a white knight, or a management buy-out in response to unsolicited pressure'.

The authors' key empirical findings were as follows:

(i) friendly targets were more likely to have been run by a founder or the founder's family; and the 'probability of an acquisition, and particularly of a friendly acquisition, rises with management ownership'.

(ii) 'synergistic' takeovers were much more likely to be friendly; whereas 'disciplinary' takeovers were more likely to be hostile. Further, consistent with prior theoretical expectations, hostile targets appeared to be 'poorer' performing firms.

(iii) compared to other Fortune 500 firms, hostile targets exhibited significantly lower Tobin's Qs (market value to replacement cost of assets), had higher debt levels; and were older, smaller, more slowly growing, invested less of their income, were less likely to be controlled by founding family, and had lower 'officer' ownership:

Low Q, low market value, low growth and investment, and the absence of a founder are the characteristics of a firm that are most likely to make it the target of a hostile bid (ibid., p. 30).

(iv) compared to other Fortune 500 firms, friendly targets were younger and smaller; but exhibited similar Tobin's Qs and growth rates. They were also more likely to be run by the founding family and to have higher officer ownership:

> The decision of a CEO with a large stake, and/or with a relationship to the founder, to retire often precipitates a friendly acquisition. High officer ownership is the most important attribute in predicting friendly acquisitions (ibid., p. 30).

Again, the work of Shleifer, Vishny and Morck represents a key empirical contribution to the literature; particularly in respect of their finding that, in line with theoretical expectations, synergistic and disciplinary takeovers were associated (respectively) with 'friendly' and 'hostile' target responses.

Mergers and acquisitions: causes and effects

Financial motivation for mergers   A series of studies has indicated that acquiring firms are more highly geared than their targets - and samples of control firms - with bidders increasing leverage post merger (e.g., Mueller, 1980; Weston and Mansinghka, 1971).

This evidence is not consistent with the 'pure financial rationale' for mergers, which postulates that real gains may accrue from mergers when the unused debt (or cash) capacity of the acquirer is profitably utilised when combined with a highly geared, cash-poor, target.

In a recent empirical study of 79 acquiring firms, (and the targets they acquired), drawn from Fortune's 1000 list for 1979, Bruner (1988) attempted to empirically test Myers and Majluf's (1984) theory that: value is created when firms with low financial gearing ('slack-rich') acquire firms with high financial leverage ('slack-poor').

In contrast to previous research, Bruner's

empirical evidence supported the hypothesis - in that prior to merger, bidders had significantly higher levels of 'financial slack' (and lower leverage) than a large sample of control firms.

Acquired companies also exhibited significantly higher leverage levels than both the control sample and their acquirers. Bruner (ibid., p. 216) concluded:

> Taken as a whole, the results are consistent with the financial economies motive for merger of the generic theories of financial change in merger. Bidders are relatively unlevered ex ante and then lever up. Merger-announcement returns are associated with these changes.

The empirical work of Bruner is the first to provide rigorous support for the pure financial rationale for mergers. It may also offer a clue (at least partly) to the determinants of the liquidation/merger alternative; in that highly levered distressed acquisition targets - though not as highly levered as failing firms - may nonetheless make attractive targets, inter alia, in consequence of the 'pure financial rationale'.

Profitability of acquisitions   In a novel empirical study, Ravenscraft and Scherer (1987a) investigated whether, as a result of the replacement of inefficient management and/or synergies, targets improve profitability performance post acquisition.

Using the financial performance data of large US corporations, disaggregated to the level of lines of business (LBs), the study was based on 95 acquisition targets, and a control sample of 2732 manufacturing LBs, drawn from the period 1975 to 1977.

Ravenscraft and Scherer's key empirical results indicated that acquired firms' pre acquisition profitability was one percentage point lower than the industry norm. Perhaps more interestingly, nine years after takeover, acquired LBs exhibited profitability levels significantly below those of non-acquired LBs which had similar market and industrial features. The authors concluded:

> Tender offer targets of the 1960s and early

1970s entered their acquirers' organisations with a profit record slightly inferior to that of their two-digit industry peers. Nine years later, on average, they performed appreciably less well. An important reason for their deteriorated post-takeover returns was the write-up of asset values stemming from the payment of acquisition premiums (ibid., p. 154).

Hence this novel study offers no evidence in support of the 'economic gains' rationale for mergers, and to that extent may be indicative of other managerial motives for making acquisitions.

Acquisitions and labour/managerial effects   Brown and Medoff (1987) provide new empirical evidence pertaining to the impact of mergers on labour and wages. Using very large samples of acquired and control firms in a Michigan Employment Security Commission databank (covering the period 1978 to 1984), the authors sought, inter alia, to discover the effects of mergers on employment and wage levels. Their main empirical findings indicated that:

> mergers are associated with wage declines of about four per cent and employment growth of about two per cent ... the common public perception of acquisition providing the occasion to slash wages and/or employment finds little support (ibid., p. 14).

In another novel study, Walsh (1988) investigated the effects of merger or acquisition on the turnover rates of 'top management', in the new combination, for five years following takeover.

The relevant theoretical literature suggested that turnover rates of top management, following acquisition, would be comparatively high because: (i) mergers breed anxiety amongst management; (ii) there may be a 'culture clash' following merger; and (iii) in consequence of the market for corporate control (above), inefficient target managers may be displaced.

Using survey responses from 55 parent companies involved in acquisitions (matched with a control sample of 30 non-acquiring firms), relating to the period 1975 to 1979, Walsh discovered that top management turnover rates following acquisition were significantly higher than those in the control sample. Furthermore, post merger turnover rates did not appear to vary with firm size or acquisition type (e.g., related versus unrelated acquisition). Walsh (p. 180) concluded:

> The description portrait alone provided a basis to discuss Drucker's (1981) 'rule' that the parent company must prepare to replace the acquired company's top management team within the first year of the acquisition ... the parent company should be ready for management turnover occurring at more than 12 times the normal rate.

Acquisitions and strategic fit   Since little (aggregate) evidence has been forthcoming in support of the purported economic gains arising from mergers, considerable research effort has been expended on classifying and analysing acquisitions according to their strategic fits (see e.g., Guth, 1985; Pekar, 1985). For example, Kitching (1967), in an early empirical study, noted that where managers had indicated a successful merger, there was a strategic fit between acquirers and their targets in terms of size and market share.

In a more recent multivariate empirical study of 218 bidding and bid-for companies, drawn from Fortune's 500 over the period 1962 to 1983, Shelton (1988) attempted to assess whether the value emanating from mergers varied with the 'strategic fit' between targets and bidders.

His key empirical findings suggested: (i) strategic fits, where either the target or bidder's assets are used intensively, create value when the fits are 'identical' (similar products and customers); or 'related-supplementary' (similar products, but new customers); or 'related-complementary' (new products, but similar customers); and (ii) 'unrelated' mergers (new products and new customers) provided the least amount of value creation: 'acquisitions that permit expansion into new markets (related-supplementary) or within the same business (identical) create the most value'.

Acquisitions and cultural fit   In relation to the
literature on acquisition and strategic fits, Hall
and Norburn (1987, p. 27) commented:

> the   impact   of   corporate   culture   on
> organisational   performance   suggests   the
> existence   of   a   further   fit   in   successful
> acquisitions, that being the fit between
> organisational values and behaviours.

Although no direct empirical evidence currently
exists in relation to mergers and cultural fits,
from related evidence, Hall and Norburn outlined
four hypotheses which suggest themselves as worthy
of future empirical validation: (i) the success of
a merger will be directly correlated with the degree
of cultural fit between participants; (ii) where
cultural   fit   is   not   evident,   the   degree   of
acquisition success will be determined by the degree
of post-acquisition autonomy granted to the target
organisation;   (iii)   acquisition   success   is
determined by the degree of post-acquisition people
planning   carried   out;   and   (iv)   successful
acquisition   will   be   associated   with   matched
expectations from the managers of bidders and
targets in terms of personnel policy, remuneration,
degree of autonomy and management style.
Hall and Norburn have thus attempted to forge a
novel link between the organisational behaviour/
industrial sociology literature and the 'success' of
acquisitions   in   terms   of   organisational/cultural
fits.   Empirical evidence on these issues is awaited
with interest.

The 'winner's curse'   Varaiya (1988) attempted to
test the 'winner's curse' hypothesis, which states
that 'in any bidding situation a party which
unknowingly overestimates the value of a given
object tends to bid higher than its competitors and
is, therefore, more likely to win it'.
Employing   multivariate   regression   analysis   on
samples of 91 US firms which made acquisitions,
(paired with their targets), over the period 1974 to
1983, Varaiya concluded:

> For a sample of corporate takeovers our results
> show that, on average, the winning bid premium

significantly overstates the capital market's estimate of the expected takeover gain ... Regression results provided support for the predicted effect of dispersion of opinion ... pre-acquisition winning buyer profitability is positively related to the magnitude of overpayment (ibid., p. 216).

Hence Varaiya's study offers interesting new evidence in respect of the premium paid to target shareholders in a competitive merger bid situation.
It has been noted that previous evidence suggests that the market 'gets it wrong' when valuing target shares (i.e., the premium paid to target shareholders is based on an overestimate of the potential gains flowing from the merger).
Varaiya's study suggests that at least part of this premium may result from a natural tendency amongst competitive bidders (with sufficient resources) to bid in excess of the capital market's 'true valuation'.

Acquisition financing   Franks, Harris and Mayer (1987) investigated the means of payment pertaining to 954 UK and 1155 US mergers over the period 1955 to 1985.
Inter alia, their empirical findings indicated that:
(a) compared to equity acquisitions, in both the UK and the US, significantly higher bid premia accrued to target shareholders involved in cash acquisitions;
(b) in a UK setting, no abnormal returns were earned by either cash or equity bidder shareholders in the month of the acquisition;
(c) in the US, there was evidence of positive gains to the shareholders of cash acquirers, and negative gains (losses) to shareholders of equity ones;
(d) in both the UK and US, post mergers returns, in the two years following acquisition, were not significantly different from zero in respect of cash acquisitions; and
(e) over a similar period, US shareholders appeared to experience abnormal losses where an acquisition was all-equity financed.
Grammatikos, Makhija and Thompson (1988) reported a theoretical model which focused on the financing decision relating to mergers - and more particularly to leveraged buy-outs. Their analysis, inter alia,

produced 'conditional predictions' which suggested:
(i) more favourable economic characteristics, in terms of expected returns, or low correlation of returns with market returns, are associated with higher debt - and lower outside equity - merger financing; and
(ii) leveraged buyouts occur where favourable economic aspects are present, in the form of a low correlation of target return with market portfolio, or where the target offers a relatively high rate of return.

Auerbach and Reishus (1988) investigated whether the choice of payment (cash/shares) in mergers and acquisitions was related to various corporate and individual tax incentives.

Based on a sample of 318 large US mergers and acquisitions, between 1968 and 1983, their preliminary empirical analysis suggested:

1. Many mergers and acquisitions provide an opportunity for corporations and their shareholders to receive some tax benefits.
2. In a small minority of cases, these benefits are large in comparison to the value of the acquired company, suggesting that taxes provided motivation.
3. Even in cases where there are significant tax benefits, there is no strong evidence that they are driving factors in the takeovers. (ibid., p.70).

In relation to means of acquisition financing and potential tax benefits, Auerbach and Reishus postulated four hypotheses for empirical verification:
(a) where high premiums are paid, or there are low shareholder bases in acquired stock, the deferment of (otherwise payable) capital gains tax will lead to the use of stock for merger payment;
(b) low book values of depreciable assets, relative to market values, should be associated with taxable (stock) transactions, in consequence of potential (depreciable) asset step-ups;
(c) substantial tax loss/credit target carryforwards should be associated with non-taxable (stock) merger financing; and
(d) the use of cash should be: 'greater when acquiring firms have not needed to go to the market

for new equity funds, and less where firms have an apparent desire to disburse cash from the corporate form'.

Employing logit regression analysis, Auerbach and Reishus's empirical results suggested:

> there is little evidence that the corporate tax effects we have identified are important in determining the form of the merger transactions ... while the current results provide no strong support for taxes as an important motivation to merge, this can only be tested directly when merged firms are compared with firms which did not merge.

Predicting acquisitions, buy-outs and sell-offs

This section reports three recent multivariate empirical studies which attempt to predict the vulnerability of firms to takeover, buy-out and divestment.

Takeover prediction

Chapman and Junor (1987), in a study of 29 acquired and 69 non-acquired Australian public companies, developed discriminant models with the aim of investigating whether a number of variables – suggested as theoretically appropriate – could differentiate between the two samples.

Using financial and market performance data, over the period 1973 to 1978, the following explanatory variables were included in their empirical models: (a) liquidity (not defined); (b) leverage (long-term debt to assets); (c) asset undervaluation (the ratio of estimated replacement value of assets – less book value – to book value); (d) valuation ratio (not defined); (e) relative growth (sales growth relative to asset growth); (f) profit margin (not defined); (g) net asset growth (the rate at which net assets grow through the issue of new equity); (h) firm size (sales); and (i) control type; with 'owner' and 'manager' control specified by reference to a number of complex criteria.

Based on these variables, their discriminant models were able to correctly identify 70 per cent of the firms in the original samples. A number of variables appeared to be significant takeover predictors. In particular, asset undervaluation was much greater amongst acquired firms; such that 'it would appear that failure to adequately revalue assets is capable of independently conveying information to prospective buyers regarding the state of the firm'.

Furthermore, illiquid, low levered, firms appeared to be more vulnerable to takeover. In addition, takeover targets exhibited significantly higher profit margins than the matched control sample. This was an unexpected result:

> We can only conclude that in the Australian corporate environment, in the period under consideration, high profit margins per se were no defence against takeover unless accompanied by prudential measures such as adequate liquidity (ibid., p. 508).

Of the remaining explanatory variables, only firm size and control type entered the discriminant functions significantly. Smaller firms appeared to be more takeover prone; and manager-controlled companies exhibited a greater vulnerability to acquisition than owner-controlled ones. Chapman and Junor (ibid., p. 513) concluded:

> The results for leverage and asset undervaluation appear to reflect the influence of persistent upward inflationary pressure and rising nominal interest rates. Thus rising interest rates may lead firms to reduce their long-term debt which, as a consequence, renders them more attractive as takeover targets. Failure to revalue is likely to be ubiquitous; the resulting asset undervaluation, however, will be acute in periods of rapid inflation and appears to convey information to acquiring firms.

Predicting management buy-outs

Maupin (1987), in a novel study of 97 US firms identified as having changed from public to private ownership (via management buy-out), over the period 1972 to 84 - matched with publicly owned firms of similar size and industry classification - developed discriminant models with the aim of identifying significant predictors of management buy-outs.

In an earlier study, DeAngelo, et. al., (1984) found that stockholders of target firms accrued significant capital gains associated with 'going-private' transactions (that is, these events were perceived by the market to be 'good news').

Maupin hypothesised the 'good news' pertaining to management buy-outs might emanate from real expected gains through: (i) a reduction in listing, registration and other stockholder servicing costs; and (ii) the introduction of an ownership structure which improves managerial incentives.

In relation to the latter potential gain, Jensen and Meckling (1976) have argued that when management ownership falls, the incentive for them to maximise returns will likewise decline; which may in turn result in a fall in firm value. Hence Maupin argued that management buy-outs, with the consequential increase in managerial equity ownership, 'reduces their incentive to shirk'.

Maupin's variables were selected after reference to questionnaire returns from 53 of the management buy-out firms. The major motivational factors proffered by these firms for buy-outs were: (a) that internal cash flows minimised the need for equity funding; (b) management and stockholders perceived that the market had undervalued the company; and (c) tax advantages were created by an increase in depreciation write-offs.

Maupin's multivariate discriminant model contained seven explanatory variables derived from data in the year preceding buy-out. These were: (1) concentration of ownership (the proportion of stock held by management and/or the board of directors); (2) the ratio of cash flow to networth; (3) the ratio of cash flow to total assets; (4) price/earnings ratio; (5) price/book value ratio; (6) the ratio of the book value of depreciable assets to their original cost; and (7) dividend yield.

The model exhibited a classification accuracy of 78 per cent in the estimation sample, rising to 81 per cent in a holdout (validation) sample. Two variables, ownership concentration and cash flow to assets, entered the model significantly (at the 5 per cent level); the remaining explanatory variables were all significant at the 10 per cent level.

A relatively high proportion of equity (54 per

cent) in buy-out target firms was owned by management, compared to 37 per cent in the control sample. Maupin considered that this result was consistent with 'the logic that the greater the percentage of stock held by management, the more easily a change to private ownership can be accomplished'.

Cash flow to total assets (and to net assets) proved to be significantly higher in buy-out firms: 'the typical company to be taken private through a management buy-out is one that has a record of generating large and steady levels of cash flow'.

Further, the mean price/earnings ratio (12.8) for buy-out firms was significantly lower than in the control sample (18.3). Maupin (ibid., p. 325) concluded:

> As suggested by managers of the ex-public firms surveyed, the relatively low stock market prices resulted in incentive programs being of less value to key personnel. The lower the stock price, relative to the potential return from successful management buy-out, the more attractive the buy-out became to managers who believed that private ownership would allow them to manage the company more efficiently and according to their own best interests.

Maupin also discovered that dividend yields were significantly higher in buy-out firms - as was the book value of depreciable assets to asset costs - with: 'a large majority of managers surveyed reporting that the significant tax advantages created by the increase in depreciation was one of the most important factors in the decision to go private'.

Finally, Maupin discovered that, consistent with prior expectations, management buy-outs were 'good news' for target shareholders; they enjoyed significant positive abnormal returns in the year preceding buy-out.

Maupin's study is an important extension to the literature concerned with predicting corporate outcomes. His rigorous research indicates that modelling techniques, which have previously been limited to corporate failure and mergers, can be usefully applied to predicting management buy-outs. In addition, his research lends strong support to the 'classical' view that higher management ownership is associated with maximising shareholder returns; in that buy-out targets had significantly lower performance levels than a control sample of firms - a characteristic quoted as being a key motivational factor by those pursuing management buy-outs.

Predicting corporate divestments

In a comprehensive seminal study of the determinants of corporate sell-offs made by large US manufacturing corporations, Ravenscraft and Scherer (1987) discovered that about one-third of US acquisitions (made during the 1960s and early 1970s), were subsequently sold-off.

Using samples of 278 fully divested lines of business (LBs), and a large control sample of 2084 non-divested LBs, Ravenscraft and Scherer developed logit models which incorporated a wide range of explanatory variables.

Some of their more general findings, derived from case studies, indicated that 'sell-off occurs in response to profit performance deemed unsatisfactory by corporate management'. A more formal statistical analysis also showed that 'the fall in profitability preceding sell-off is not primarily a result of industry-wide shocks, as distinguished from matters more directly under the control of operating-level management'.

In total, the final specification of their empirical model contained no less than 21 explanatory variables (suggested as theoretically appropriate). Their key empirical findings were:
(i) the profitability of divested LBs (operating income to assets) was significantly lower than non-divested LBs - after holding other factors constant, a change in profitability from fourteen to minus one per cent (i.e., loss-making), increased the probability of divestment by as much as seven per cent.
(ii) case study evidence also indicated that some divestments were triggered by a parent company being financially distressed, necessitating the raising of funds through the sale of 'good' businesses. This was supported by Ravenscraft and Scherer's empirical models, which showed that relatively high parent company profitability exerted a negative influence on sell-off.
(iii) Ravenscraft and Scherer concluded that LBs

with a relatively high market share are 'likely to be viewed as strategically advantageous, inhibiting sell-off'; a proposition which was fully supported by their empirical evidence.

(iv) their evidence indicated that the probability of sell-off was significantly higher for intensive research and design LBs: 'presumably because research and design investments support the expectation of future quasi-rents'.

(v) a change of management in the parent company, in the two years preceding divestment, increased the probability of sell-off: 'apparently because new brooms attempt to sweep clean, and/or emotional commitments to past decisions are broken'.

(vi) contrary to expectations, liquidity appeared to be higher in divested LBs. Ravenscraft and Scherer concluded:

> evidently sell-off was more apt to be induced by poor company profitability than by a weak working capital position or high leverage ... the single year variable suggested that sell-off is induced by a series of low returns, and not simply by poor LB profitability in one year (ibid., p. 185).

The Ravenscraft and Scherer study represents an important, novel and rigorous contribution to the literature. Their results are particularly interesting in the context of the current study, especially their finding that 'sell-off was on average a manifestation of financial distress'.

Summary

This chapter has examined the copious evidence pertaining to the determinants and impact of mergers, management buy-outs and corporate divestments.

In general, the extensive empirical literature on the rationale for, and effects of, mergers appears to support the new 'managerial' theories - rather than shareholder wealth-maximisation ones - though some new empirical evidence did indicate a 'pure financial' rationale for US acquisitions. Nonetheless, the 'sources' of merger gain (if any) still remain elusive and largely unexplained.

Interesting attempts to extend traditional failure/merger empirical modelling techniques, to predicting corporate divestments and management buy-outs, were also outlined. In particular, and germane to the current study, empirical models indicated that US corporate divestments were predominantly 'a manifestation of financial distress'.

6 Corporate failure: cause and cure

Introduction

It was noted in Chapter 1 that although a plethora of corporate failure prediction models have been published in recent years, the development of the theory/causes of corporate collapse has advanced very little (see e.g., Scott, 1981; Wadhwani, 1984).

Although failure prediction models are now used widely by credit/investment analysts (indeed a Z-score model is currently available on Datastream), the financial/explanatory variables included in them have tended to be selected on the basis of 'statistical fitting', rather than on a comprehensive theory of corporate decline.

The purpose of this chapter is to review the existing theory/evidence on the causes of, and the associated symptoms relating to, corporate collapse - and the appropriate 'cures' advanced in the turnaround literature - before examining recent advances in modelling techniques which, inter alia, attempt to incorporate 'theoretically appropriate' explanatory variables into failure prediction models.

Chapter 7 includes a section outlining the empirical/theoretical limitations of failure/merger prediction models.

Corporate failure: the causes

This section outlines a number of studies which attempt to explain/isolate the underlying causes, and associated symptoms, of corporate collapse (rather than merely identifying the financial ratios which, ex post, reflect these characteristics when failure is imminent).

A later section examines the efficacy of failure prediction models which incorporate a number of 'secondary causal' variables specified in these studies.

The experts' views

In recent years a large number of articles/books have been published by journalists/academics and other acknowledged experts, containing their views, often based on case studies and/or practical experience, relating to the causes of corporate collapse.

Barmash's study   Barmash (1973) made an early attempt to isolate the major causes of corporate collapse.   Based on 15 case studies of 'great business disasters', he concluded that 'the basic cause of business disaster is greed, human greed, simple and unadulterated.   In most cases, the greed crossed over the line into corruption'.

However, Altman (1983), quoting from a 1980 Dunn and Bradstreet survey, noted that only about 0.5 per cent of US corporate failures were connected with fraud; the vast majority (94 per cent) were associated with 'managerial problems'.

Ross and Kami's study   In another early study Ross and Kami (1973), after referring to a number of well known business failures, also concluded that 'bad management' was the fundamental cause of corporate collapse.

From evidence gleaned from case studies, Ross and Kami advanced 'ten commandments' which must be adhered to if corporate failure is to be avoided:

(1) there must be a corporate strategy which is clearly communicated;
(2) there must be corporate control systems;
(3) the board of directors must actively participate;
(4) there must be no one-man (autocratic) rule;

(5) there must be management in depth;

(6) management must be kept informed and be able to respond to change;

(7) the customer should be treated like a king;

(8) computer misuse should be avoided;

(9) the accounts must not be manipulated; and

(10) organisational structure must meet people's needs.

As with Barmash's study, no concrete empirical evidence was proffered in support of the 'ten commandments' hypothesis. Indeed, a list of the ten predominant causes of corporate failure, articulated by Cohen (1973) in a similar study, bears little resemblance to those from which the 'ten commandments' are derived.

<u>Smith's study</u>   Based on evidence gleaned from several case studies, Smith (1966) was one of the first authors to list the perceived causes of corporate collapse (and was also the first to identify the 'autocratic' manager as being a key factor).   Smith concluded that the key factors responsible for corporate failure were: (i) the autocratic manager; (ii) resistance to change; (iii) lack of control; (iv) overdiversification; (v) decentralisation; and (vi) bad luck.

It will be noted that the first three causes specified by Smith are similar to those identified in Ross and Kami's study.

However, for the purpose of predicting corporate failure, it appears obvious that even if one were to accept that some of these symptoms are associated with individual business failures, it must be the degree of severity with which they operate, and/or a particular mix of factors, which is responsible for eventual corporate demise.   From a failure prediction perspective, therefore, a multivariate modelling approach is clearly indicated.

For example, many of the most successful companies are run by 'autocrats'.   Indeed the successful autocrat is often 'head hunted' to effect corporate turnarounds - and yet 'one man rule', or the 'autocrat', is specified in almost all studies as being the key causal factor associated with corporate collapse.

The practitioners' views

The opinions of practitioners pertaining to the

causes and symptoms of corporate failure offer another interesting insight into the factors responsible for corporate collapse; particularly as they deal, on a day to day basis, with the 'sharp end of the problem'.

Spotting danger signals   From his vast experience of business rescue and corporate turnarounds, Homan (1984), national director of insolvency services for Price Waterhouse UK, and chairman of Price Waterhouse World Firm International Insolvency Advisory Group, noted that:

> Z-score analysis cannot distinguish the company with dynamic new management dedicated to a turnaround from the company in which bad managers are firmly entrenched. Hence formulae such as the Z-score should be used as a screening device only. They can be invaluable in screening a large number of accounts, but there can be no substitute for common sense and sound business judgement in spotting potential trouble (p. 33).

Homan considered that the root causes of corporate collapse could be considered under four main headings:
(i) weaknesses in management. Homan considered this to be a predominant cause of business failure. The most common problems are: (a) succession in a 'family' business by incompetent relatives; (b) a dominant chief executive - particularly when no obvious successor has been groomed; (c) management being 'out of its depth' in a rapidly expanding business; (d) high quit rates amongst key employees; and (e) a reluctance by managers to invest their own capital in the business.
(ii) technical/commercial problems. Homan was of the view that even 'competent' management may be 'wrongfooted' by the increasing pace of technical and political change: 'a business with volatile products or markets, susceptible to changes in costs, fashion, technology, social attitudes, overseas competition or exchange rates is clearly vulnerable'.
(iii) faulty accounting. Homan noted that 'no company can monitor its progress (or lack of it) effectively without accurate financial information'.

Early warning signals of faulty accounting include a qualified audit report; changes in accounting policies; and late, or untimely, reporting of corporate accounts.

(iv) financing problems. Homan considered that highly geared firms, or businesses with 'a capital structure weighted to short term maturities', are prime failure candidates. Other danger signals include the payment of dividends in a loss-making situation, and the granting of increasing security to obtain credit.

Homan listed 16 'danger signals' associated with corporate failure, which, though appearing frivolous, he noted 'in reality they are anything but frivolous':

(1)   personalised number plates on the Rolls;
(2)   a company flagpole;
(3)   a fountain in the forecourt;
(4)   a fish tank in the board room;
(5)   a statue of the founder in reception;
(6)   beautiful new offices;
(7)   a beautiful new secretary;
(8)   a company yacht/aeroplane;
(9)   a fast-talking managing director;
(10) directors who use military titles;
(11) obsession with tax avoidance;
(12) too many board papers;
(13) no accountant on the board;
(14) too many auditors;
(15) too friendly with their banker;
(16) too many bankers.

Homan stated that: 'the first seven or eight can indicate management pre-occupied with prestige rather than profit and the existence of excessive overheads. Others may include the lack of a proper balance of skill or lack of information available to the board'.

Although, as Homan admitted, some of the items specified in his list appear frivolous (and nebulous), they do illustrate the inherent difficulties involved in attempting to isolate the early warning signals/symptoms linked to the causes underpinning corporate collapse.

Anticipating corporate collapse   McMillan (1984), managing partner with Arthur Anderson, concluded that:

Insolvency is not strictly a problem which has its origins in recession. In fact the majority of failures ... were on tracks leading to insolvency well before the recession came along. The seeds were set in place by business decisions to overtrade, whether by expanding too fast in the principal business activity, or by getting involved in other business activities that took management beyond either their field of competence, their capacity to manage, or their financial ability to service the related debt.

In relation to annual accounts, McMillan suggested that the following points should be addressed when evaluating potential failure signals: (a) were they presented on a timely basis?; (b) were they audited?; (c) was the auditor the same as in the previous year?; (d) was the auditor's opinion clean?; and (e) were the assets revalued?

McMillan was also of the view that liquidity problems were a symptom of 'management having come close to its absolute limit of capability'. This results either from the business outgrowing the capability of the management team in numerical terms; or the business outgrowing the capacity of its information system to generate vital information for managers on a timely basis.

Finally McMillan noted that 'overconcentration' was a key factor explaining corporate failure:

Although the expanders are more risk burdened than the constant performers ... the latter is also not immune to business problems. Its management may not be imaginative, may already be at its limit of competence ... and may not recognise that it is being overtaken by competition, or that its product or service is being superseded by advances in technology. While the former could result in a takeover and no exposure to creditors, it may not and the sudden shock that comes through obsolescence may be too severe to assure recoveries for lenders (p. 12).

As with previous authors, McMillan listed a number of 'serious danger signals' indicative of impending corporate collapse: (i) excessive dividends; (ii) multiple banking arrangements; (iii) fluctuating profits; (iv) an increase in overheads; (v) product/production problems; (vi) delays in receipt of goods; (vii) changes in accounting principles; and (viii) loans or advances to directors, shareholders or affiliates.

Further warning signals   From his professional experiences, Norgard (1987), international director of KMG Financial Reorganisation Services, suggested that business failure stems predominantly from 'poor management':

> well managed businesses weather economic storms, poorly managed businesses sink ... Too often the company that demonstrates poor management has deeper problems; lack of proper financial information, no business development plan, inadequate product mix, or an inability to respond to changes in the business environment. These companies are also inclined to be reactive rather than innovative when confronted with problems (p. 44).

According to Norgard, 'poor management' often results from: a domineering executive; inadequate management depth; an unbalanced administrative team; an uninvolved board; and a weak finance function.

So far as warning signals are concerned, Norgard posited that 'a business on the road to failure exhibits signs well in advance of its actual demise'. He grouped the symptoms into operational and accounting aspects. In relation to operational problems the signals are: overtrading; margin erosion; the big project; high gearing; corporate inertia; changes to the business; problem borrowing; decline in service standards; undercapitalisation; and 'too easy money'.

The accounting signals include deteriorating financial ratios; lack of cash flow forecasting; lack of financial information; and creative accounting.

Forecasting 'bad times'   Based on a study of 120 organisations - 'healthy, sick and deceased' - Boocock and Drozd (1982), management consultants with Touche Ross, attempted to build a 'forecasting' model of corporate decline, based on an assessment of three levels of management performance: executive, middle and operational.

For example, at level one (executive) an assessment of a company's management structure should be undertaken for signs of management rigidity, a management team spread too thinly/weighty, the degree of management knowledge of the industry, and its knowledge of 'sound management techniques'.

Other areas for review include whether the company has adequately defined objectives (and strategic planning); the ease of entry into the industry in which the firm operates; and the level of reliance on individual suppliers.

The second (middle management) assessment involves 'a review of the company's planning process and its monitoring and control systems, its acknowledgement of, and reaction to, inflation, and its financial trends'. Finally, at level three, an analysis should be conducted relating to an organisation's productivity and profitability characteristics.

Although Boocock and Drozd make an interesting attempt to formulate a 'scoring system', with the purpose of gauging the likelihood of failure flowing from the 'secondary symptoms' of managerial incompetence, their 'weighting system' was not disclosed; and thus it is impossible to assess the subjective weights they attribute to each 'managerial problem' identified (and also to the relative weights attached to each level of analysis).

Argenti's study of corporate collapse

Argenti (1976) was the first author to critically review the (then) prevailing evidence on the causes and symptoms of corporate collapse.

Based on the available evidence of a number of 'writers and experts', his own experiences, and a number of detailed case studies, Argenti produced an interesting and stimulating analysis of the causes and symptoms of corporate decline. He concluded that 12 major elements (in italics) are linked together to cause corporate failure:

If the management of a company is poor then two things will be neglected: the system of accounting information will be deficient and the company will not respond to change. (Some companies, even well-managed ones, may be damaged because powerful constraints prevent the managers making the responses they wish to make). Poor managers will also make at least one of three other mistakes: they will overtrade; or they will launch a big project that goes wrong; or they will allow the company's gearing to rise so that even normal business hazards become constant threats. These are the chief causes, neither fraud nor bad luck deserve more than a passing mention. The following symptoms will appear: certain financial ratios will deteriorate but, as soon as they do, the managers will start creative accounting which reduces the predictive value of these ratios and so lends greater importance to non-financial symptoms. Finally the company enters a characteristic period in its last few months (p. 122).

Argenti expanded on the twelve causes/symptoms as follows:

(1) Management   Argenti noted that 'there is a wide or even universal agreement that the prime cause of failure is bad management'. The 'defects' include: one-man rule; a non-participating board; an unbalanced 'top team'; a weak finance function; lack of management depth; and where the chairman is also the chief executive.

(2) Accounting information   Argenti was of the view that 'what is lacking in companies that fail is accounting information'. He noted four predominant indicators: lack of budgeting control; inadequate product costing systems; and incorrect asset valuations.

(3) Change   Argenti concluded that 'the more serious the defects in the top management structure of a company, the higher will be the chances that two vital omissions will be made in running the company: the information system will be deficient and, vastly more important, the company will not adequately respond to change'.
Argenti identified five main areas where an inadequate response to change is apparent: in relation to competitive, political, social, economic

and technological environments.

(4) Constraints   Argenti posited that the growing emergence and power of corporate stakeholders (e.g., consumers, the state and employees), the increasing power of the media, and pressure from trade unions and other pressure groups, exerts severe constraints on a firm's strategic decision-making processes; and thus contributes to their decline.

(5) Overtrading   Argenti stated that a poorly managed company is also more likely to commit the 'gross error' of overtrading. This surfaces in two ways: where management fails to estimate the amount they need to borrow, or do not allow sufficient time to arrange loans to finance expansion; and where management increases turnover at the expense of margins.

(6) The 'big project'   Argenti's definition of a 'big project' includes diversification programmes, acquisitions, internal expansion and the launch of a new product/service. From case studies, he concluded that 'one of the almost tediously repetitive mistakes that leads to failure is the big project where costs are underestimated or revenues overestimated'.

(7) Gearing   It has been noted in previous chapters that high corporate gearing (leverage) has consistently been shown to be a key factor ultimately responsible for corporate failure. In this respect Argenti concluded that:

> Poorly managed companies tend to gear up their equity beyond the prudent level so that their company is vulnerable not just to massive errors or strokes of gross misfortune, but even to the normal hazards of business (p. 136).

(8) Normal business hazards   So far as normal business hazards are concerned, Argenti stated they could never amount to a valid excuse for failure: 'a manager who blames an economic recession for his company's collapse is like a captain who has not heard the weather forecast'.
  Hence, although Argenti considers that 'bad luck' can cause failure, he considers it a rare cause, bad

management again being considered the key factor.

(9) Financial ratios   Argenti expressed serious doubts about the usefulness of ratios in predicting corporate failure (at least when used exclusively). However, in his later (1983) work he did admit that they may be reliable indicators in the last two years before collapse.

(10) Creative accounting   Again, Argenti draws attention to the fact that creative accounting is a symptom not a cause of corporate failure: 'almost all companies that are not healthy do attempt to conceal the truth in their published accounts and all ratios calculated from them are unreliable'.
According to Argenti, some of the key creative accounting techniques include: delay in publishing annual accounts;   capitalising research costs; payment of dividends from equity or loans; reduced expenditure on routine maintenance; leasing and hire purchase arrangements; treatment of ordinary income as extraordinary;   and subsidiaries increasing dividend flows to the parent company.   ·
However, Tweedie (1989), in a recent paper pertaining to creative accounting and current financial reporting practices, drew attention to the fact that 'window-dressing' of corporate results is now widespread, even amongst relatively successful companies.
It appears that a 'follow my leader' approach is being adopted by many firms; in that companies which are 'healthy' are (nonetheless) utilising creative accounting techniques in an attempt to match competitors' reported results, rather than to just 'hide' imminent prospects of failure.
Hence, creative accounting no longer appears to be the exclusive domain of ailing enterprises - and to this extent its usefulness as a potential explanatory variable in failure prediction models may be impaired.

(11) Non-financial symptoms   According to Argenti, the non-financial indicators of corporate collapse include: price cuts; a decline in quality of the firm's service/product;   tightening of credit policies; running down of stocks; resistance to employee pay increases;   delays in capital expenditure authorisation; a declining market share; and a growing volume of customer complaints.

(12) The last months   Argenti's case studies
suggested that in the last few months before failure
'the number and severity of the symptoms rapidly
increase. The stock market will by now certainly
have marked the shares down, perhaps to a fraction
of their previous level'.

Argenti's study of the causes and symptoms of
corporate collapse represented a landmark in the
study of failure prediction. It was the first to
attempt to synthesise the extant literature (as well
as new evidence) into a rational theoretical
corporate failure framework.
A later section will describe how researchers have
attempted to incorporate some of the causes/symptoms
described by Argenti as explanatory variables in
failure prediction models.

Slatter's turnaround study

Slatter's (1984) study of the causes of corporate
decline, and associated turnaround strategies,
represented a second landmark in the development of
a more comprehensive theory of corporate decline.
Based on case study evaluations of forty UK
companies which were in 'turnaround situations',
Slatter's book contains, inter alia, a comprehensive
analysis (similar to Argenti's) of the underlying
causes of corporate collapse. (Indeed there is a
large measure of agreement between Argenti and·
Slatter on the fundamental causes of corporate
failure).
Slatter's list of the principal causes of
corporate collapse, with the percentage frequency
with which they occurred in his sample given in
parenthesis, were as follows:

(1) Lack of financial control (75);
(2) Inadequate management - including one-man rule,
    neglect of core business and lack of management
    depth (85);
(3) Lack of, or inadequate, price and product
    competition (58);
(4) High cost structure, relative to competitors
    (83);
(5) Non-response to changes in market demand (58);
(6) Adverse movements in commodity markets,
    including interest rates (30);
(7) Operational marketing problems (22);
(8) The big project, where costs are underestimated

and/or revenues overestimated (32);

(9) Acquisitions: the acquisition of 'losers' (firms with weak competitive positions); payment of an unjustified high price; and poor post acquisition management (15);

(10) Financial policy in the form of high gearing, a 'conservative' approach, and inappropriate financing sources (20); and

(11) Overtrading (0).

In relation to his list of the causes of corporate failure, Slatter (p. 55) concluded:

> From my analysis, it appears that a crisis situation is likely to occur most frequently when a firm, already weakened by poor management, lack of control and inefficiency, is subjected to adverse movements in market demand and commodity prices, price competition and to 'one-off' problems resulting from the so-called big project.

From evidence gleaned from his case studies, Slatter also listed ten major symptoms of corporate decline which indicate that a company needs to implement turnaround strategies: (a) decreasing profitability; (b) decreasing real sales; (c) increasing debt; (d) decreasing liquidity; (e) a restricted dividend policy; (f) 'accounting practices' in the form of 'window dressing', delays in publishing accounts and a change of auditors; (g) top management 'fear'; (h) rapid management turnover; (i) declining market share; and (j) lack of planning/strategic thinking.

Like Argenti's earlier work, Slatter's detailed study has been influential in the choice of non-financial variables included by researchers in failure prediction models.

Determinants of failure trends

The results of an early empirical study by Altman (1971) indicated that corporate bankruptcy rates vary across industries and in response to changes in the economy as a whole. In the UK, for example, Wadhwani (1984) has shown that corporate insolvency rates are positively correlated with the rate of inflation. Staw, Sandelands and Dutton (1981) have also argued that corporate failure is more probable in situations of 'sudden environmental decline'.

Hudson (1987), in a study of 1,830 UK companies which failed between 1978 and 1981, attempted to analyse their characteristics in terms of age, region and industrial structure.

His sample was partitioned on the basis of creditors', members' and compulsory liquidations. He discovered that most liquidated firms were newly formed, with the highest risk period lying between the first and ninth year of incorporation: 'it would appear to take a period of nine years before one can think of a company as being established in the sense of it not being at special risk of becoming insolvent. However, there does appear to be an initial honeymoon period, with few firms becoming insolvent in their first two years'.

This finding was consistent with Hudson's prior expectations, in that he considered that time may act as a filter between viable and unviable firms; but that an initial honeymoon period endures until creditors become aware that a company cannot meet its debts.

Additional analysis indicated that firms in the manufacturing sector were less likely to fail within the first three years of incorporation; whereas high unemployment in depressed regions was 'linked with the closure of long-established firms, with the resulting loss of a large number of jobs'. Furthermore, as the recession deepened, 'the proportion of long-established firms closing tended to increase'.

Hudson's study makes an important contribution to the literature, in terms of explaining the economy-wide factors responsible for companies entering liquidation proceedings; particularly his finding that young firms, between two and nine years of age, exhibit a significantly higher prior probability of failing.

Small business failure

In a recent study of the causes of small business failure, London Business School (LBS, 1987) surveyed 100 clearing bank managers to obtain their views on the perceived factors responsible for the failure of a sample of 437 UK business start-ups.

The sample consisted of businesses, within their first five years of start-up, which failed in 1985/6, stratified by age of failure and industrial sector.

The questionnaire forwarded to bank managers contained a list of 26 possible 'dimensions of failure'. Respondents were requested to indicate whether they considered each dimension represented a primary (integral) or contributory (associated) causal factor. The full list of factors, together with the percentage frequencies mentioned for primary (P) and contributory (C) factors, was as follows:

(1) Undercapitalisation (P: 54, C: 77);
(2) Poor operation's management (P: 29, C: 57);
(3) Poor management accounting (P: 26, C: 60);
(4) Short term liquidity (P: 26, C: 54);
(5) Poor chief executive (P: 23, C: 57);
(6) High gearing (P: 23, C:50);
(7) Poor state of local economy (P: 16, C: 35);
(8) Poor marketing/sales management (P: 16, C: 54);
(9) Theft and dishonesty (P: 16, C: 18);
(10) Bad debts (P: 11, C: 27);
(11) Increased competition (P: 8, C: 40);
(12) Other personnel reasons (P: 8, C: 9);
(13) Loss of vital personnel (P: 6, C: 17);
(14) Obsolete product (P: 6, C: 15);
(15) Other management reasons (P: 6, C: 8);
(16) Poor quality product (P: 5, C: 21);
(17) Poor facilities and machinery (P: 4, C: 25).

On average, each business had no less than seven failure dimensions, of which three were primary. Initial undercapitalisation and poor operation's management, however, appeared to be the most common integral factors.

Relative to other industrial sectors, fewer manufacturing concerns failed in their first year of existence, but suffered a higher death rate in their fifth year following start-up. In relation to corporate failure and business age, the authors concluded:

The age of the business at failure did affect the kinds of problems which would cause failure. It seems that management reasons generally become more important over time, as do production and labour-related problems. The importance of the loss of vital personnel and disputes between directors decreases, while financial problems show a U-shaped trend being most important in the first, fourth and fifth years (ibid., p. 37).

Given the large number of businesses failing within the initial seven years following their incorporation (Hudson, op. cit.), the results of the LBS study offer interesting new evidence pertaining to the perceived reasons for the failure of small business start-ups.

It is also interesting to note that the authors reported that: 'our respondents thought that the failure of the business was unavoidable in nearly half of all the industry sectors, with retailing and professional services being particularly vulnerable'.

Conclusions

A common theme running through the studies reviewed in this section has been that the major cause of corporate failure is explained in terms of 'plain bad management' (particularly evidenced by 'one-man rule', or the autocratic chief executive).

So far as modelling (or predicting) corporate failure is concerned, however, it is difficult to perceive, a priori, how 'bad management' could be correctly specified, other than through the many articulated 'symptoms' that accompany it.

Another problem is that although an ex post autopsy of failing firms may reveal, for example, than on average 'one man rule' was present, many highly successful companies are also ruled by autocrats. Hence a key question which might then be posed is what factors are responsible for the successful/unsuccessful autocrat?

From a modelling perspective, it follows that a multivariate approach is indicated, to capture the widest range of 'bad management' early warning signals (symptoms) to test for their relative importance (significance).

Although, from the studies reviewed, there is some measure of agreement on the symptoms of corporate decline, only rigorous empirical verification of the large number of factors specified will throw further light on the predominant causes of corporate failure. In this sense the 'theory of corporate collapse' is still in its infancy.

Corporate failure: the cures

Given the often nebulous and/or superficial nature of the causes of corporate failure advanced in the extant literature, it is not too surprising that relatively little effort has been expended on developing a comprehensive (theoretical) set of measures designed to prevent corporate collapse (Argenti being one of the few exceptions).

Instead, much of the research in this area has stressed the 'cures', or turnaround strategies, which are designed to effect a restoration of health. For example, Bibeault (1981), who surveyed 81 chief executives involved with turnarounds, devoted much of his book to describing cures in terms of organisational and human factors. Finkin (1987), in a similar study, also stressed the need to establish new values and priorities in a turnaround situation: 'this means a new corporate culture, which must quickly permeate the operating environment'.

Hence, like the theory of corporate collapse, the (linked) theory underpinning corporate turnaround (the 'cures'), is also still in its infancy.

Preventing corporate collapse

In relation to his study of the causes of corporate collapse, and the associated cures, Argenti (1976) is one of the few authors who attempted to: 'summarise the minimum measures that companies should take. Unlike the advice to managers found in most textbooks, this is not a recipe for achieving success; it is one for avoiding failure'.

Argenti's preventive measures, which matched his exposition of the causal factors, were as follows:

Top management   On the commencement of business, duplication of management skills should be avoided; and more particularly firms should 'take a strong finance man into the top team'. Gaps in managerial ability below board level should also be avoided; and 'above all, make sure that when a company grows beyond a certain point - the rules for identifying it are not known but it is nevertheless recognised - make sure that one-man rule is gradually diluted'.

Accounting information   Budgets, cash flow and costing exercises should be implemented. Argenti considered that if management is not familiar with these techniques: 'it is difficult to see how they can avoid making mistakes in pricing products, in launching projects, in closing down activities, in calculating savings from a merger - and a hundred other decisions'.

Response to change   Argenti postulates that basic planning procedures, which are outlined in the strategy literature should be adopted by firms to enable them to respond to change.

Gearing   Since a company becomes vulnerable to normal business hazards when its gearing reaches a specific level, as a preventive measure Argenti advises: 'never allow loan interest to reach a certain level at which the company's cash flow is threatened if a normal business hazard does occur'.

Overtrading   Argenti suggested that constraints should be operated to avoid the tendency of managers to overtrade: 'entrepreneurs, proprietors and managers all have one thing in common - they worship growth, expansion, size, big numbers, empires'.

Big projects   Argenti considered that the big project should be avoided: 'few managers would be so foolish as to launch a project that is so big that it will bring the company down. The problem is that costs become so much higher and revenue so much less than originally envisaged that this brings the company down'.

In relation to his 'survival kit', Argenti (ibid., p. 182) concluded:

I do not wish to labour the point but the philosophy ... is that managers are as much responsible for avoiding failure as for achieving success. To set a challenging target, to devise a strategy to achieve it, and to monitor progress towards it, is now a routine of good management. To set a minimum acceptable target, to devise a strategy to ensure it will be exceeded, and to monitor that one's company is not failing is, I believe, the urgent new criterion of good management.

Turnaround strategies

In recent years a growing number of books (e.g., Bibeault, 1981; Finkin, 1987; Kharbanda and Stallworthy, 1987; Kibel, 1982; Slatter, 1984) and articles (e.g., Hofer, 1980; Hambrick and Schecter 1983; Schendel, Patton and Riggs, 1976; Taylor, 1983) have been published outlining strategies to turn around ailing enterprises.

Given that there is no integrated framework pertaining to the causes of corporate collapse, it is not too surprising that no accepted definition of what constitutes a 'turnaround situation' has emerged in the literature. For example, Kharbanda and Stallworthy (1987) defined it as being 'when a company looks as though it will fail in the near future'; Schendel, et. al., (1976) defined it in terms of a decline in real net profit for four or more years; and Slatter (1984) used the term to refer to firms or operating units 'whose financial performance indicates that the firm will fail in the foreseeable future unless short-term corrective action is taken'.

In this respect it is interesting to note that Altman (1983) describes how his failure prediction Z-score model was 'successfully' utilised to 'proactively' effect a corporate turnaround by a US firm.

This section briefly describes two of the more influential turnaround studies, before examining some recent empirical research pertaining to the implementation of turnaround strategies.

Slatter's strategies

From evidence gleaned from detailed case studies, Slatter (op. cit.) formulated 'ten generic strategies which firms commonly use, alone, or in combination, to effect corporate recovery'.

(1) <u>Change of management</u>   Slatter was of the opinion that since 'inadequate top management is the single most important factor leading to decline, most turnaround situations require new chief executives'.

(2) <u>Strong central financial control</u>   Slatter was of the view that 'the introduction of strong central financial control at the beginning of a turnaround is virtually a law'.

(3) Organisational change/decentralisation Slatter noted four situations where this form of strategy may be necessary: (i) for divestment of part of a business; (ii) to enable the chief executive to gain effective management control; (iii) to effect structural change in large companies; and (iv) to divisionalise highly centralised firms.

(4) New product-market focus Where a fundamental cause of a company's decline lies in its lack of competitiveness in particular product-market segments: 'it is imperative that the firm refocus its overall product-market strategy if sustainable recovery is to take place'.

(5) Improved marketing The evidence accumulated by Slatter led him to conclude that 'turnaround firms characterised by poor management rarely - if ever - have a well executed marketing plan,' with selling and pricing being the most common marketing mix elements focused on in turnaround situations.

(6) Growth via acquisition Slatter noted that a common recovery strategy implemented in turnaround situations is growth through acquisition:

> Acquisitions are most commonly used to turnaround stagnant firms not in a financial crisis but whose financial performance is poor. The objective of growing by acquisition ... is related to the faster speed at which turnaround can be achieved by following the acquisition route (ibid., p. 96).

(7) Asset reduction Slatter was of the view that asset reduction 'is often part of product-market reorientation'. In addition, for severely financially distressed firms: 'the adoption of an asset-reduction strategy may be the only viable option left open to a firm'.

(8) Cost-reduction strategies These are indirectly aimed at increasing cash flows via measures to increase profit margins; and are usually targeted at loss-making operations.

(9) Investment strategies Slatter noted that this strategy was most commonly implemented by companies which acquired turnaround firms; where the strategy is aimed at 'reducing costs through the replacement of worn-out or obsolete plant and equipment, or at promoting growth, either organically or via acquisition'.

(10) Debt restructuring strategies   This form of turnaround strategy is usually adopted by a 'firm that has reached a cash flow crisis, is usually overgeared, and must reduce its debt/equity ratio to acceptable industry levels before the firm can be said to have recovered financially'.

Argenti's trajectories

Argenti (1976) considers that there are three identifiable trajectories, or routes, which firms follow to insolvency. Hence the turnaround strategies, or 'cures', he advocates vary according to which path ailing firms are pursuing.

Type 1 trajectory   Type 1 firms follow 'a very low profile, indicating that their performance never rises above poor before sinking into the arms of the receiver'. Argenti believed this type of failure trajectory was unique to newly incorporated, small, firms. So far as effecting a cure is concerned, Argenti concluded:

> Can anything be done to save the company, or a worthwhile part of it, once it begins to fail? I think not. Remember that it fails, usually, because the proprietor has very seriously overestimated the revenues or underestimated the costs of his project. Not just by a fraction, by a whole world. By the time he discovers his mistake I believe it is always too late to arrange a takeover or to cut back or economize or boost sales significantly (ibid., p. 171).

Type 2 trajectory   Type 2 firms 'shoot upwards to fantastic heights before crashing down again'. Since Argenti considers the key cause associated with this type of failure is one-man rule, the cures he advocated are based on implementing various controls (or checks and balances) on chief executives. These included: banks placing representatives on the board; banks taking on equity stake in the business; and pressure to appoint an 'independent' chairman.

Type 3 trajectory   According to Argenti, firms which follow this trajectory are mature and larger; and in which 'we only become interested at the end of a period of good to excellent performance, when there is a partial collapse, followed by a plateau, after which there is a rapid decline into insolvency'.

One of Argenti's fundamental cures for this type of 'waterlogged' firm is the implementation of effective corporate planning. However, before the plateau is reached, Argenti advocated:

> the banks or shareholders or younger managers or stakeholders or government should insist on a fundamental change of management together with secure but controlled retrenchment or the sale of unprofitable activities or of property or other assets. Or seek to be taken-over (ibid., p. 176).

Empirical evidence on turnarounds

Using business periodicals to subjectively attribute the causes of decline, and of the subsequent turnaround, of 54 US firms which exhibited four consecutive years of real net income decline, Schendel, et. al., (1976) classified turnaround strategies into 'operational' and 'strategic' ones.

They discovered that declines caused by strategic factors (e.g., absolute products) tended to be associated with strategic cures (e.g., new product innovation); whereas operating factors (e.g., labour problems) were likewise associated with operational cures (e.g., cost controls). The authors concluded:

> The key to turnaround is a well formulated concept of strategy and a strategic planning process that can discern whether it is existing operations that must receive attention, or whether the basic business must be reformulated. The firms studied were able finally to make these distinctions and where they used the formal tools of strategic planning, they were

able to change strategy and regain income patterns (p. 11).

In a later empirical study, Hofer (1980), after studying a sample of 12 'underperforming' firms, also classified turnarounds into strategic and operational groupings. His findings also lent support to the former study, in that there was some correlation between the causal factors associated with 'downturns' and the type of cure implemented for the turnaround.

For example, companies operating below breakeven levels tended to implement more radical asset-reduction and revenue increasing strategies; whereas those operating closer to breakeven levels pursued less onerous cost-cutting strategies.

Perhaps the most comprehensive empirical study of turnaround strategy, in mature industries, was that recently conducted by Hambrick and Schecter (1987).

Data was drawn from the PIMS database on 260 mature businesses which displayed an average pretax return on investment, over two years, below ten per cent.

Using twelve strategically defined variables, the authors attempted to test a number of propositions - suggested, in the main, by Hofer (1980) and Bibeault (1982): (i) among mature businesses, short-run turnaround success is associated primarily with retrenchment and efficiency moves, not entrepreneurial moves; and (ii) 'a variety of successful turnaround gestalts, or sets of moves, can be observed', including cost cutting, asset reduction, product/market refocusing and revenue generation.

From their empirical analysis the authors concluded:

The cluster analysis indicated three primary successful turnaround gestalts: asset/cost surgery, selective product/market pruning, and piecemeal strategy ... It was found that the choice among these three strategies was associated with certain characteristics of the business ... Asset/cost surgery was pursued primarily by businesses with low levels of capacity ultilization; selective product/market pruning was undertaken primarily by businesses with high levels of capacity utilization; and piecemeal strategy was followed primarily by businesses with high market share (ibid., p. 247).

The Hambrick and Schecter study is the most comprehensive (and rigorous) empirical study of turnaround strategies to date; and tended to confirm the early case study work of Hofer (1980).
However, as with the 'theory' of corporate collapse, the authors concluded that 'both theoreticians and practitioners need framework and evidence for thinking about responses to poor organisation performance'.

Predicting corporate collapse

Given that much of the theory, and supporting evidence, pertaining to corporate collapse has been 'speculative' and/or 'anecdotal' in nature, a number of researchers have attempted to empirically verify some of the 'causal factors' specified by Argenti, et. al., by including 'non-financial' variables in failure prediction models (either alone or in combination with conventional financial ratios).
This section describes a number of recently published failure prediction studies which investigate whether these causal factors (variables) are more accurate predictors of corporate failure than conventional financial ratios; and/or whether they are more timely indicators of corporate collapse.

Quoted company failure prediction

In a preliminary empirical study, Peel, Peel and Pope (1985) attempted to assess how efficiently seven non-financial, or qualitative, variables could discriminate between 34 failed and 44 non-failed UK industrial quoted firms.
The variables were constructed from information contained in annual accounts and reports, and were modelled with direct reference to the causal factors specified by Argenti, et. al., in the extant failure literature. The variables covered the following aspects of corporate behaviour.

<u>Timeliness of reporting</u>   As noted in preceding sections, a number of authors have noted that

companies approaching corporate failure often delay publication of the 'bad news' contained in their annual accounts.

Since a lengthening reporting lag (e.g., compared to the previous year's lag) can be observed before the accounts, and the financial information contained therein, are actually published, the timeliness with which annual accounts are reported is (potentially) a particularly useful indicator of impending collapse.

However, given that it is generally accepted that directors can directly influence the reporting lag, they may actually improve (shorten) the lag if they perceive that the market would otherwise perceive a lengthening lag as 'bad news' - and hence directors could 'confuse' the market - the information content of the variable may thus diminish and/or might prove transitory in nature.

Notwithstanding this, the variable might still retain some informational content; since it has been noted that at least part of a lengthening reporting lag may be 'involuntary' - that is, it is not subject to the influence of directors, in that for firms in poor shape: 'the auditing process may be particularly problematic and time consuming' (Ohlson, 1980).

Peel, et. al., collected two variables relating to the timeliness of corporate reporting: the time lag (in months) between a company's financial year end and the date it published its annual accounts (in the year preceding failure); and the change in the reporting lag (in months) from the previous year.

The authors stressed that the latter variable might prove to be a particularly useful predictor, since it may be changes in reporting behaviour which more accurately reflect (or signal) impending collapse - rather than the level of reporting lags.

Directors' shareholdings   It was noted earlier that Homan (1984) suggested a potentially useful early 'warning signal' of corporate collapse is 'a reluctance by managers to issue their own capital into the business'.

Peel, Peel and Pope suggested that if directors are viewed as being in a privileged position with regard to price sensitive corporate information, then any change in their shareholdings may correlate with impending good or bad news not yet formally disclosed in corporate reports (see Peel, 1985).

The variable employed by the authors in their

empirical study to model this potential signal was the change in directors' aggregate beneficial ordinary shareholdings in their company (as a proportion of issued equity), over the two accounting periods preceding corporate failure.

<u>Board changes</u>   Peel, et. al., argued that as corporate failure approaches, changes in board composition should increase.

For example, director resignations may signal the 'abandonment of a sinking ship', or, alternatively, may indicate shareholder dissatisfaction with managerial performance - which may in turn reflect dissatisfaction with corporate performance.

Director appointments, on the other hand, may be indicative of expanding operations and/or an attempt to strengthen an 'inadequate' management team.

Furthermore, Keasey and Watson (1987) have noted that 'a company with an autocrat in control is more likely to experience an outflow of managerial personnel as failure approaches'.

The variables employed by Peel, et. al., to capture changes in board composition, over the two accounting periods preceding failure, were: directors resignations as a proportion of board size, a similar variable to reflect director appointments; and changes in these two variables in the two accounting periods prior to corporate collapse.

Peel, Peel and Pope's empirical analysis suggested, in relation to the previously specified variables, that a number of statistically significant differences existed between their samples of failed and non-failed (control) firms.

In particular, relative to non-failed firms, failing companies, on average, were typified by a significantly longer reporting lag in the year before failure; by an increasing reporting lag relative to the previous year; by a declining proportion of corporate equity owned by directors; by a higher frequency of resignations over appointments (and therefore a net decline in board size); and by an increasing frequency of resignations in the year before failure, compared to the previous year.

Multivariate logit models, containing various combinations of these variables, also proved to have significant discriminatory ability - with the timeliness of annual accounts exhibiting the highest explanatory power.

Peel, Peel and Pope concluded: 'it is clearly possible that these variables may enhance the predictive power of financial ratios and therefore one suggestion for future empirical work is that they should be combined with financial ratios'.

Peel, Peel and Pope (1987), in a later study using the same samples, did combine a number of traditional financial ratios with the non-financial ones used in their earlier research. Further, the predictive power of their various multivariate logit models was tested on inter-temporal holdout samples.

In all, 17 logit models were reported, which incorporated various combinations of the financial/non-financial explanatory variables. Their main empirical finding was that the addition of non-financial variables, particularly the time lag in reporting annual accounts, to conventional financial ratios did indeed enhance the explanatory power of failure prediction models both within and out-of-sample.

The empirical findings of these two studies were the first to support some of the hypotheses advanced by Argenti, et. al., pertaining to the underlying causes of corporate collapse - particularly those relating to the reporting behaviour of financially distressed firms.

Private company failure prediction

In a study of 56 of the largest private UK industrial companies to fail, between 1980 and 1985, matched with 56 similar non-failed (control) firms, Peel (1987) attempted to assess whether two non-financial variables added to the explanatory power of conventionally estimated non-quoted failure prediction models.

The new explanatory variables were: (i) the timeliness of reporting of annual accounts; and (ii) whether an auditor's going concern qualification had been issued in the last published accounts before failure.

Eleven multivariate logit models were estimated from the original samples; with their classification accuracy tested on similar holdout samples comprising 12 failed and 24 non-failed firms.

Some preliminary analysis indicated that the average reporting lag for the failed firms (13 months) was significantly longer than for the non-failed companies (8.6 months). Hence although the reporting requirements for UK quoted and private firms differ under the Companies Acts (see Peel, 1985), failing firms in both classes appear to exhibit significantly longer reporting lags than their non-failing counterparts.

It appears, therefore, that the conventional wisdom advanced in the literature, pertaining to the reporting behaviour of ailing enterprises, is fully supported by empirical evidence in respect of both quoted (public) and private UK companies.

Peel's logit estimates, for example, clearly indicated that the addition of the reporting lag variable, to groups of conventional financial ratios, led to an improvement in both the explanatory and predictive power of his private failure prediction models.

However, the issuance of an auditor's going concern qualification, in the last accounts before failure of private firms, did not appear to be a significant predictor of corporate collapse.

Indeed, the sign on the coefficient of this variable (positive) appeared perverse; in that it was associated with the survival of private UK companies rather than their demise (see Peel, 1989, for further discussion of this variable).

Small company failure prediction

Keasey and Watson (1987) made a substantive and comprehensive contribution to the failure prediction literature, in respect of testing a number of Argenti's hypotheses on small UK firms.

Keasey and Watson's data set comprised 73 failed and 73 non-failed single plant independently owned firms, trading in the North East of England, between 1970 and 1983. In addition, further samples of 10 failed and 10 non-failed firms were used as holdout samples.

The main purpose of their study was to test whether a number of non-financial variables, modelled with respect to hypotheses generated in the Argenti study, had predictive content in small company failure prediction models - either alone or in conjunction with conventional financial ratios.

In particular, a number of qualitative variables were collected in an attempt to capture the early symptoms of corporate collapse which emanate from: defects in management structure; the inadequacy of accounting information systems and factors effecting audit lags; the manipulation ('window dressing') of financial statements; and factors associated with high gearing levels.

Some of Keasey and Watson's more interesting univariate results suggested:
(i) a minority of failing firms experienced a significant net outflow of directors, as failure approached, compared to non-failing firms;
(ii) on average, failing firms exhibited significantly longer reporting lags (14 months), relative to the control sample (9.3 months);
(iii) relative to non-failed firms, failing ones received a higher number of audit qualifications in their last set of available accounts; and
(iv) failing firms, on average, were more likely to have loans secured against assets than non-failed ones.

Keasey and Watson's multivariate logit estimates indicated that although models containing only financial ratios performed at a similar level to models containing only non-financial ones, models containing a combination of the two variable sets performed best of all (in terms of classification accuracy and explanatory power).

More specifically, their logit models indicated that the probability of small companies failing was higher: the longer the reporting lag in annual accounts; the fewer the number of directors; and where banks had secured loans against the firm's assets. The authors concluded:

> The results while being of a tentative nature, indicate that marginally better predictions concerning small company failure may be obtained from non-financial data as compared to those which can be achieved from using traditional financial ratios. The variables selected and the signs of the coefficients generally support the Argenti hypotheses concerning the process of corporate failure (p. 331).

Implications

Substantial progress has been made in UK failure prediction research regarding the modelling of the non-financial symptoms of corporate distress.

In particular, it is encouraging that in relation to different populations of firms (quoted, private and small), the timeliness with which firms submit their annual accounts appears to be a highly significant predictor of corporate collapse - that is, longer reporting lags are associated with corporate decline - strongly supporting the observations of Argenti and other practitioners.

However, much research remains to be completed in this area - more specifically, a much larger number of non-financial indicators requires investigation.

In addition, a much longer time period (e.g., 10 years) before collapse also requires examination - to ascertain whether non-financial variables act as 'early warning signals' (or precursors) to the more obvious deterioration in financial ratios shortly before failure.

Downward spirals and corporate collapse

In a novel study, Hambrick and D'Aventi (1988) attempted to formulate a new theoretical model (partly based on previous research, and partly based on their own empirical findings) to explain the failure, or 'downward spiral', of 57 large publicly traded US corporations over the period 1972 to 1982.

The failing firms were matched with 57 non-failed ones on the basis of size, industry and product/market mix. Data was collected for up to ten accounting periods before failure.

Hambrick and D'Aventi noted that no integrated theory existed in relation to explaining large-scale corporate collapse; but that a review of related literature suggested four key constructs of corporate decline:

(i) <u>Domain initiative</u>   The literature on corporate decline (e.g., Hannan and Freeman, 1984; Miller and Friesen, 1977) suggested that an examination of a company's level of domain initiative - or the degree to which it changes its markets or products - should be central to any study of corporate collapse.

Various measures were used by Hambrick and D'Aventi to capture domain effects. These included: the number of wholly and partially owned units and subunits acquired or formed; and the number of four-digit SICs added by a company.

(ii) <u>Environmental carrying capacity</u>   Hambrick and D'Aventi noted that both ecology and strategy theorists (e.g., Andrews, 1971; Tushman and Anderson, 1986) held the view that: 'the environment plays a major role in affecting the fates of firms. The environment provides the organization's resources and creates contingencies with which the organization must deal'.

Hence strategists have argued that corporate failure is more probable in times of 'sudden environment decline' (see e.g., Harrigan, 1980; Staw, Sandelands and Dutton, 1981).

Hambrick and D'Aventi posited that the environment's 'carrying capacity' - the ability of the environment to support a population of firms - is a key factor explaining corporate failure. The variable used by the authors in their empirical analysis to proxy this effect was a measure of 'real demand growth', based on industrial SIC growth.

Organisational slack This construct was originally specified by Cyert and March (1963) as being the surplus of resources in excess of those required to maintain an organisation's 'coalition' - that is, 'a cushion of actual or potential resources' (Bourgeois, 1981).

Although the exact causal relationship between 'slack' and corporate collapse is still subject to considerable debate in the literature, one school of thought (e.g., Singh, 1986) posits that it is positively associated with 'innovation, improved decision making and, hence, with survival'. Another view (e.g., Bozeman and Slusher, 1979) is that 'reduced slack, or scarcity of resources, induces managerial paralysis'.

The authors collected a number of variables in an attempt to proxy these effects. These included a firm's equity to debt ratio, and working capital as a proportion of sales.

Performance criteria Hambrick and D'Aventi noted that corporate performance is related to organisational slack, in that 'to the extent the organization performs poorly - especially in terms of profits - its slack will be depleted'.

Hence they sought to establish whether large business failures are characterised by long or short periods of 'performance deficiency' in the years before failure - using the after tax return on total assets as their performance variable.

Employing univariate analysis, and multivariate logit models, on data up to ten years before failure, Hambrick and D'Aventi's key empirical findings were as follows:

(i) the 'bankrupt' sample showed signs of relative weaknesses (in terms of slack and performance) as long as ten years before failure. It appeared that 'poor profits limit any increase in equity (via retained earnings) and cause the firm to take on more debt to finance operations'.

So far as 'immediate slack' (working capital to sales) is concerned, the 'bankrupts' exhibited a relative decline only in the year preceding failure.

(ii) in terms of 'new domain' and 'location growth', no significant differences were apparent between the failed and non-failed firms in each of the ten years preceding collapse.

However, failing firms exhibited significantly higher levels of 'vacillation' (variability) in domain initiative: 'the persistence and strength of the pattern for new domains alone support the view that failure is accompanied by excesses or imbalance - either doing too much or too little'.

(iii) the authors found no significant differences between the failed and non-failed firms' environment carrying capacity in any of the ten years before failure.

Hence they concluded that 'bankruptcies generally did not occur in contexts of long-term environmental decline. The view of failure occurring in chronically depressed industries was not borne out in the data'.

From the evidence of their own empirical study, and related theory and evidence, Hambrick and D'Aventi formulated a new theoretical framework in an attempt to explain the 'downward spiral' of large organisations into eventual collapse. The theory is characterised by four distinct phases:

1. Origins of disadvantage   This occurs in excess of a decade before eventual collapse. It is a period (not examined empirically by the authors) when 'the seeds of weakness are sown'; in that by year ten before failure the eventual bankrupts 'already have lagging levels of slack and profitability'.

2. Early impairment   The second phase occurs between years ten and six before failure. In this phase a failing firm moves 'from viable levels of slack and performance to being marginal'.

3. Marginal existence   The third phase, between

149

years six and three before failure, in the downward spiral is characterised by the firm 'hovering in a breakeven state'.

Hambrick and D'Aventi's empirical results suggested four tendencies emerge in this period: (a) extreme strategic behaviour (inaction or hyperaction); (b) vacillating strategic behaviour; (c) the carrying capacity of a firm's environment 'is neutral, even buoyant'; and (d) the working capital position of failing firms is similar to that of non-failing ones.

4. **Death struggle** The final two years in a large failing firm's existence is characterised by: continuing extreme (and vacillating) strategic behaviour; a significant and abrupt environmental decline; and by a sharp deterioration in slack and performance prior to ultimate demise.

From the new empirical evidence collected in their study, Hambrick and D'Aventi concluded:

> On average, large firms have a very substantial period of warning, and hence of potential turnaround, before they fail. That these bankruptcies were culminations of ten-year declines is compelling testimony to organizational inertia, perpetual error under stress ... or suggestive of remarkably long strings of bad luck. Conversely, the relatively long process of decline suggests that turnaround managers may generally have more time to conduct their task than is often thought (p. 20).

The Hambrick and D'Aventi study makes a key and substantial contribution, both theoretically and empirically, to the extant literature aimed at explaining the dynamics and processes underpinning large company corporate collapse.

More specifically, their finding that the seeds of corporate collapse are sown in excess of a decade before failure is a crucial one - in so far as modelling the 'initial causes' of failure is concerned - particularly as most previous studies have concentrated their efforts on the period immediately preceding collapse.

Hence, inter alia, the Hambrick and D'Aventi study indicates that, in relation to large company failures at any rate, the search for the origins, or initial triggers, of corporate collapse should focus on corporate behaviour at least ten years before eventual formal failure.

Some modelling extensions

This section outlines two new empirical studies which attempt to extend traditional corporate failure prediction techniques to provide a more sophisticated modelling approach than has previously been employed in this area of research.

Failed and 'grey area' firms

In a study of 194 large private UK industrial firms, drawn from Extel's unquoted companies service between 1982 and 1985, Peel and Peel (1987) attempted to assess how efficiently failure prediction models could discriminate between financially distressed firms which entered insolvency proceedings and ones which survived (continued to trade).

More specifically, previous corporate failure prediction research has been largely based on partitioning companies into discrete groups of failed and 'sound' or 'healthy' ones (see e.g., Taffler, 1984, for a review of the literature).

Since a potential model user would be more interested in, or obtain more utility from, differentiating between firms which will eventually fail and those which appear financially distressed (or in the 'grey area') but which will continue to trade (recover) - rather than the more obvious fail versus healthy dichotomy - the main aim of Peel and Peel's study was to analyse the ability of failure prediction models to accurately identify so called 'grey area' firms.

Employing logit and multilogit statistical techniques, models were estimated from data derived from samples of 56 'healthy' (profit making) firms; 56 failed (liquidated) companies; and 34 non-failed (loss-making) firms - where the latter group, a priori, was intended to represent companies in the 'grey area'.

Using financial and non-financial variables derived from the last accounts before failure, Peel and Peel's main empirical findings were as follows:
(i) although logit models based on the failed and non-failed loss-making samples exhibited significant

discriminatory power (R²: 0.28), their ability to classify, relative to traditional models (R²: 0.60), was considerably impaired.

For example, a logit model derived from the failed and loss-making samples correctly identified 79 per cent of the firms in the original estimation sample, but only 58 per cent in a holdout validation sample. Comparative figures for models based on the failed and 'healthy' samples were 88 per cent and 89 per cent respectively;

(ii) multilogit models, derived by analysing the three samples simultaneously, did not improve the classification ability of the dichotomous logit models based on the healthy and loss-making firms;

(iii) in all cases, the logit and multilogit models displayed their highest classification error rates amongst the failed and loss-making firms.

Hence, Peel and Peel's analysis suggested that the predictive accuracy of previously reported failure prediction models may have been heavily overstated. In particular, models based on financially distressed (but solvent) firms and failed (insolvent) ones, exhibited (correct) classification rates only marginally superior to those than would have been expected on a random choice selection basis. The authors concluded:

> It would appear from these results that, using conventional predictors, more general statistical techniques cannot solve the problem of accurately predicting the fate of so called 'grey area' firms. The solution to the problem (if one exists) would appear to require that additional predictors should be found (p.64).

Predicting the timing of failure

Using data over three accounting periods before failure, Peel and Peel (1988) attempted to address the problem of predicting when a company will fail, rather than (just) whether it will fail.

Previous researchers, using data one or more periods prior to corporate collapse, have estimated separate models for each period and then applied the individual models to holdout samples to determine which one displays the best fail/non-fail classification ability - with no obvious time rationale for the user.

Indeed some model builders (e.g., El Hennawy and Morris, 1983; Lincoln, 1984) have reported that discriminant models, based on data up to five years before failure, out-perform those based on data closer to failure.

For example, in a recent empirical study of small company failure prediction, Storey, Keasey, Watson and Wynarczyk (1987) reported that their 'most promising' models were based on data three or four years before failure and expressed 'dissatisfaction' because 'none of the models addressed the question of when, as opposed to whether, a firm will fail'. They concluded:

a final criticism of existing studies is that they exhibit a lack of concern with the process of failure. Indeed we are not aware of any studies that have attempted to determine when a business will fail as apposed to whether it will fail. In our view, a concern with the former question would lead to a greater emphasis upon the process of failure which we believe to be a most fruitful area for analysis (p. 236).

Hence, using multilogit analysis, the main aim of Peel and Peel's study was to investigate whether it was possible to discriminate (simultaneously) between non-failed (solvent) firms and failing companies one, two and three reporting periods before failure - and thus combine the information content of 'traditional models' to generate a predicted (probability) failure time horizon.

The models were estimated from financial data derived from a sample of 79 UK quoted industrial firms, and tested on an inter-temporal holdout sample of 27 similar firms.

The multilogit estimates produced four predicted probabilities for each company - which summed to unity - namely, that it would remain solvent, or that it would fail one, two or three reporting periods into the future.

The model proved to have significant classificatory ability across the four potential outcomes (R^2 = 0.33) - with an overall four-group predictive accuracy of 72 per cent, rising to 77 per cent in the holdout sample.

Although the error rates displayed by the multilogit model were comparatively high in respect of years two and three before failure, the new modelling technique adopted by Peel and Peel was an innovative first attempt to solve the 'if and when' problem encountered by traditional model builders.

Summary

The purpose of this chapter has been to review the existing theory and evidence pertaining to the causes and symptoms of corporate failure - and the associated cures and turnaround strategies - as well as recent related advances in the corporate failure prediction literature.

In contrast to the comprehensive theory developed in respect of mergers and takeovers discussed in Chapter 5, the theory of corporate decline has received scant attention in the literature and remains relatively unchartered.

However, some recent attempts have been made to develop a more integrated framework in respect of the underlying causes and symptoms of corporate collapse. In particular, Argenti, Slatter and Hambrick and D'Aventi have made key contributions in this respect.

Their efforts have resulted in a new line of empirical research which has investigated, inter alia, whether a number of non-financial, or qualitative, variables enhance the explanatory power of traditional (financial ratio) failure prediction models.

Although this work is still in its infancy, it is encouraging that a number of new empirical studies do appear to verify that a selection of 'theoretically specified' variables have significant explanatory power in a corporate failure setting.

To the extent that the (limited) theoretical framework now emerging in respect of the underlying causes of corporate failure tends to centre around 'bad management', rather than macro factors or 'sheer bad luck', it may be that a fruitful area for future research, in a liquidation/merger setting, is in the context of understanding the mechanisms of 'disciplinary takeovers' - or the 'replacement of incompetent management' hypothesis.

More particularly, a pertinent question which might be addressed in future research is: if corporate collapse is caused by 'bad management', why are a large number of companies 'permitted' to enter liquidation proceedings, rather than being subjected to disciplinary takeovers when they are still going concerns?

Answers to this, and related questions, concerned with the market for corporate control, and the efficiency with which it operates, remain the subject of future research.

7 An overview

Some general observations

Using UK corporate financial data, the main aim of
this book has been to provide some new empirical
evidence on the determinants of the
liquidation/merger alternative, set against the
background of recent theoretical and empirical
developments in the corporate failure and merger
literature.

Chapter 1 provided an introduction to the theory
and evidence pertaining to corporate failure and
takeovers - and stressed that these two areas of
research have developed almost exclusively along
separate lines. Chapters 5 and 6 expanded on these
themes. In particular, it was noted that the theory
and evidence relating to mergers is much more
developed and comprehensive than is that pertaining
to corporate failure.

Notwithstanding this, statistical models, based
mainly on accounting data, appear to be more
successful in predicting corporate failure than they
are in correctly identifying takeover targets.

Given that the theory of corporate failure is
still in its infancy (Chapter 6) - whereas that
pertaining to mergers is significantly more
comprehensive, mature and sophisticated - it may at
first sight appear perverse that failure prediction

models dominate takeover ones in terms of classification accuracy and explanatory power.

However, a closer examination of the facts supports a logical explanation:

(i) although the theory of corporate collapse is underdeveloped (Chapter 5), financial ratios, at least shortly before failure, appear, on average, to be reliable indicators of impending liquidation/ receivership.

Hence, even though the literature on corporate collapse focuses, in general, on 'bad management', without specifying a comprehensive theoretical framework to identify exact causal factors, the 'economic dimensions' of corporate failure are much more readily captured in financial ratios.

In effect, relatively little is understood about the underlying causes of corporate collapse, but because the symptoms of corporate failure will be (eventually) reflected in financial ratios, this lack of theoretical understanding has not impinged on the development of 'successful' failure prediction models.

(ii) in contrast, although the theories pertaining to mergers and acquisitions are more mature and sophisticated (Chapter 5), systematic empirical testing of them has produced conflicting results, and, on average, tends to support a 'no real gains' scenario - lending indirect support to the new managerial theories of the firm.

Hence a recent line of research on the rationale for mergers and acquisitions has concentrated on organisational behavioural, 'people' and cultural issues (see e.g., Buona and Bowditch, 1989; Hunt, 1988; Napier, 1989).

In consequence, it is not too surprising that takeover prediction models, which rely on corporate accounting data, are outperformed by their failure prediction counterparts; since the 'economic dimensions' of takeovers, if a pure economic rationale even exists, are unlikely to be accurately reflected in traditional financial ratios.

These observations are also germane to statistical models designed to predict the liquidation/merger alternative outcomes - the focus of the new empirical work presented in this book.

Some specific observations

The search for a rationale as to why certain

financially distressed companies are rescued from corporate collapse by a timely merger (Chapter 2), was triggered by Dewey (1961) who emphasised that most mergers simply involve a transfer of assets from ailing to thriving firms.

Manne (1965), in a seminal paper, provided a rationale for such takeovers in terms of the operation of the market for corporate control - where managers of profit-maximising firms compete to acquire 'badly managed' ones and/or where managers of the acquiree are not attempting to maximise shareholder wealth.

Manne's theory subsequently gained much support in the academic literature - in that it outlined an economic rationale for takeovers which did not rely on traditional models based on cost minimisation and/or price increases, emanating from synergies and the creation of monopoly power, respectively.

However, Manne's theory does not explain why all financially distressed firms are not acquired - assuming that their financial predicament results from 'bad management' (as indicated in Chapter 6) - particularly when their net asset values are still positive (see Lee and Barker, 1977).

Explanations as to why some financially distressed firms have been 'permitted' to fail, rather than being subjected to 'disciplinary' takeovers, have concentrated on two main areas:

(i) <u>Market inefficiency</u>   It has been argued that, like any other market, the market for corporate control may suffer from a number of inefficiencies (e.g., in respect of information flows and 'signalling').

In consequence, potential 'disciplinary' takeover targets may be 'missed', and hence allowed to progress into liquidation proceedings. For example, after reviewing a number of recent empirical studies on acquisition and merger policy, Fairburn and Kay (1989, p. 29) concluded:

> We have argued that the market for corporate control is a decidedly imperfect mechanism for imposing discipline on weak management - expensive and inefficient. But it is the principal mechanism which currently exists. If policy is to restrain such mergers further, it should do so only if other ways of achieving managerial accountability are fostered ... the

strengthening of non-executive directors, the more active involvement of institutional shareholders, the possible development of audit committees and supervisory boards.

(ii) Managerial choice   Pastena and Ruland (1986) posited that a major factor responsible for the failure of the market for corporate control, emanated from the exercise of target management's discretion, based on the divorce between ownership and control, to pursue (in their own interests) the liquidation alternative in preference to the takeover option (which will always be preferred by target shareholders).
As was noted in Chapter 2, Pastena and Ruland's empirical results certainly appeared to suggest that 'the self interests of managers seems to be at least partly responsible for the merger/bankruptcy choice'.

Notwithstanding the debate pertaining to the efficacy with which the market of corporate control operates, its practical implications have been recognised in terms of US merger policy. As was noted in Chapter 2, under US antitrust laws an otherwise unlawful merger may be permitted on public interest grounds if it can be proved that one of the participants would otherwise fail.
Although no explicit defence, on this ground, is currently available under UK monopoly and merger legislation, it is interesting to note that the Office of Fair Trading, in a recent booklet on merger procedures (OFT, 1985, para. 20), offers the following guidance:

A company may argue that it can no longer survive independently and that the only way to keep the business alive is to sell out to a competitor. The Office may be told that the case is so urgent that an investigation by the Commission would entail closures and loss of jobs. In such cases the Director General will seek to advise the Secretary of State on the practical effects which a reference could be expected to achieve - particularly in terms of competition and of employment. Firms advancing the failing firm argument will be invited to substantiate it.

Finally, it is worthwhile to note that a significant proportion of takeover targets appear to be acutely financially distressed when acquired. For example, the new evidence presented in this book indicated that about 17 per cent of all UK quoted acquired firms in the 1970s fell into this category - a similar proportion to that found in a number of previous US empirical studies.

Key empirical results

Although the new empirical evidence presented in this book is subject to a number of methodological limitations (below), the key results to emerge suggest the following interpretation:

(a) Financial distress levels   On the basis of traditional financial ratios, measuring various aspects of corporate performance over the two accounting periods preceding failure/acquisition, financially distressed firms which failed appeared to be more acutely distressed than ones which were acquired.

Hence, on average, and not surprisingly, companies which were not the subject of a 'disciplinary' takeover, and which were thus allowed to fail, were more acutely distressed than those rescued by a timely acquisition.

This empirical finding may appear, a priori, obvious; but it is nevertheless a key one, since it suggests that the decision to acquire an ailing enterprise may not be independent of the extent of its financial distress level.

However, this does not imply that firms which eventually failed were not acquired simply because they were, at all times, too acutely distressed to make attractive acquisition targets. Obviously, at some stage, these firms, on their downward trajectory to failure, will have passed through the (average) lower distress level of those firms which were acquired.

The pertinent question then becomes: what factors were responsible for the choice of acquisition candidate, given similar distress levels, of those firm which (eventually) failed and those which were acquired? The answer to this question remains unanswered and hence the subject of future research.

(b) Managerial discretion   On the basis of the data

and the variables employed in this study, no evidence was found to support Pastena and Ruland's contention (Chapter 4), which appeared to be empirically validated by US corporate data, that some financially distressed companies escape disciplinary takeovers because certain managers prefer liquidation to the merger alternative - and (presumably) are able to successfully deter hostile bids and/or to successfully contest them.

(c) Corporate size and tax incentives   It has been argued that smaller ailing firms may make attractive acquisition targets because, inter alia, of the greater tax benefits associated will them (Scott, 1977).

However, Pastena and Ruland's empirical results (Chapter 2) indicated that, in fact, financially distressed firms which were acquired were significantly larger than ones which failed.

In contrast, the empirical results emanating from the current study suggested that there was no significant difference in size between UK distressed firms which failed and those which were acquired.

In addition, variables employed to proxy potential tax loss carryforwards also proved to be insignificant predictors of the liquidation/merger alternative. It was argued in Chapter 2 that the a priori logic of tax carryforwards as potential explanatory variables was unclear; since more acutely financially distressed firms (that is, those closer to failure), are more likely, if anything, to have larger tax loss carryforwards.

In any event, the relative value of potential tax loss carryforwards should be reflected in the price paid for the acquisition target; rather than in the initial decision whether or not to acquire.

Methodological limitations

A number of methodological limitations and problems are worthy of mention; both in relation to failure/merger studies in general, and to the current study of the liquidation/merger alternative in particular.

Some general limitations

Some common methodical problems faced by researchers, who attempt to design statistical

models to predict between various corporate outcomes, include the following:
(a) most model builders rely on historical accounting data which by its nature reflects past 'economic' events and may be subject to 'window dressing'.

In addition, the application of different accounting concepts may lead to inconsistencies in reported performance figures. Further, asset valuations based on book values may bear little resemblance to their market values.

These problems have led a number of researchers to concentrate on share price data, or 'event' studies, to assess market reaction to failure/mergers (see e.g., Fairburn and Kay, 1989).
(b) the samples from which corporate failure/merger prediction models are derived are, in most cases, not randomly selected from the populations that they are meant to represent and/or are equal in size.

This form of sampling results in biased model estimates, and also to an overstating of a model's ability to predict between corporate events (see Palepu, 1986).
(c) in validating the predictive ability of failure/mergers models, the cut-off probability points applied to samples of holdout firms are often selected arbitrarily - without giving cognisance to a decision-maker's pay-off matrix (see Altman, 1983; Palepu, 1986).
(d) most published failure/takeover prediction models are 'naive'; in that even if the problems specified in relation to historical accounting data could be surmounted, it is doubtful that financial ratios would be able to encapsulate all the significant economic dimensions of an enterprise (and certainly not the 'non-economic' ones).

In respect of failure prediction studies, however, some progress has been made in the search for non-financial variables which may predate historical accounting ratios, as explanatory variables, and thus act as 'early warning signals' of impending corporate collapse.

In addition to the previously specified problems, most studies of corporate failure and mergers (including this cne), rely on static, rather than dynamic, models to predict between various corporate events.

Hence, in most cases, only one year's data is employed to estimate the models, which usually relates to the last accounting period preceding acquisition/failure. However, some recent studies have experimented with changes in explanatory variables; and others are investigating a time span of up to ten years before failure/takeover (see e.g., Hambrick and D'Aventi, 1988; Pope, Morris and Peel, 1988).

Some specific limitations

A number of methodological problems specific to the current study are also worthy of mention:
(i) perhaps the main empirical limitation of the study emanates from the inherent difficulties involved in accurately sampling a sub-set of UK quoted acquired firms which were 'acutely financially distressed' when taken-over.

This study relied upon three well known, a priori, criteria relating to corporate profitability, short-term liquidity and whether or not an auditor had issued a going concern qualification.

However, the use of different financial criteria may well have resulted in the selection of a different sample, and hence to different empirical results.

There appears to be no easy route to circumvent this problem, since in any liquidation/merger alternative study the selection of 'financially distressed' acquisition targets must, to a certain extent, rely on 'subjective' criteria imposed by the researcher.

Notwithstanding these sampling problems, it was encouraging, in relation to the current study, that an ex post evaluation of the sample of distressed acquired firms, with a failure prediction model (chapter 4), appeared to (largely) vindicate the ex ante sampling criteria.
(ii) the models reported in this study relied, in the main, on financial ratio variables derived from accounting data in the year preceding failure/acquisition. However, in the context of investigating the determinants of the liquidation/merger alternative, access to an inter-temporal data set would have been more preferable.

In addition, no data was collected, in respect of both the failed and distressed acquired samples, to ascertain the relative frequency of abandoned and contested bids in each sample. The collection of this data would have been particularly useful in the context of investigating the 'management discretion' hypothesis discussed earlier.

(iii) the variables employed to proxy managerial discretion effects, tax loss carryforwards and relative share price movements were somewhat crude and simplistic.

Hence, until more sophisticated predictors have been incorporated into the analysis, the hypotheses which these variables attempted to test empirically, cannot be totally refuted.

Finally, the data set from which the empirical models were derived is an historical one (1971-79), and hence any conclusions flowing from the empirical analysis may not pertain in today's corporate environment.

Suggested areas for future research

A number of areas, many of them related to the limitations inherent in this study, suggest themselves as deserving of future research in a liquidation/merger context:

(i) an examination of the financial and non-financial characteristics (e.g., corporate structure) of the acquirers of financially distressed acquisition targets to ascertain whether the perceived motivation for such takeovers is based on traditional synergy/monopoly power theories; and/or whether the rationale is related to the market for corporate control/'disciplinary' acquisitions (e.g., by conglomerates).

(ii) a more comprehensive investigation of the efficiency with which the market for corporate control operates - particularly as it pertains to contested and abandoned bids in respects of failing and financially distressed acquired firms.

(iii) the use of larger samples of companies, from the current time period, to facilitate a more comprehensive examination of factors such as: the financial/non-financial profiles of companies over a longer time period (say ten years) before acquisition/failure; an investigation of share price residuals over this period; and an evaluation of changes in board and corporate structure for the period under analysis (e.g., changes in directors, divestments and reconstructions).

(iv) a re-examination of the Pastena and Ruland model of managerial discretion as it operates in a liquidation/merger context. More particularly, future research in this area might usefully concentrate on:

(a) a more sophisticated approach to modelling owner versus managerial controlled firms;
(b) a similar approach to modelling the value of directors' equity in their company (e.g., including share-options); and
(c) an investigation of the fate of directors in failed firms, compared to those in distressed acquired ones, in terms of employment/re-employment - either in the post acquisition combination, or with other companies following liquidation/takeover.

Concluding comments

As has been noted by other researchers (Ravenscraft and Scherer, 1987, p. 210):

> there are surely more opinions on why mergers are made than there are economists who have written on the subject. This may be inevitable, since merger motives are complex, and multiple motives may be at work in any given decision.

The purpose of this book has been to report some new empirical evidence, rather than just mere opinion, on the determinants of the liquidation/merger alternative, and to provide a platform from which further research might be launched.

The fact that only a handful of previous studies have been published on this topic, perhaps bears testimony to the inherent difficulties involved in attempting to model the liquidation/merger alternative.

It is the author's hope, however, that the current study will be amongst the first of many to examine the interesting link between corporate failure and mergers - particularly bankruptcy avoidance as a merger incentive - and the efficacy with which the market for corporate control operates in this context.

Appendices

Appendix 1:   Primary data

Key:

T-1   =   data taken from last accounts prior to
          merger/failure.

T-2   =   data taken from preceding year's accounts.

All variables refer to T-1 unless otherwise
specified.

FF   =   funds flow (earnings before interest, tax
          and depreciation)

TU   =   turnover (sales)

NPBT =   net profit before tax

SPH   =   highest quoted share price for each
          company for year T-1

SPH1 =   highest quoted share price for each
          company for year T-2

SPL	=	lowest quoted share price for each company for year T-1
SPL1	=	lowest quoted share price for each company for year T-2
SEH	=	Stock Exchange All Share Price Index high matched to each company for year T-1
SEH1	=	Stock Exchange All Share Price Index high matched to each company for year T-2
SEL	=	Stock Exchange All Share Price Index low matched to each company for year T-1
SEL1	=	Stock Exchange All Share Price Index low matched to each company for year T-2
BS	=	number of directors on board (board size)
DR	=	total aggregated directors' remuneration at T-1
DR1	=	total aggregated directors' remuneration at T-2
DS	=	total aggregated number of ordinary shares held by directors at T-1
SSH	=	total number of all ordinary shares held by substantial shareholders (10%+)
NS	=	total number of issued ordinary company shares at T-1
NS1	=	total number of issued ordinary company shares at T-2
CL	=	current liabilities
CA	=	current assets
TA	=	total tangible assets (CA + fixed assets)
IND	=	industry classification: 1 = predominantly manufacturing; 0 = non-manufacturing
AQGC	=	whether (1) or not (0) an auditor's going concern qualification had been issued

LAG	=	the time lag in lunar months (no. days/28) between the date of the firm's account year end and the date the accounts were published (as indicated in Extel cards)
TL	=	total liabilities (CL + long-term debt)
WC	=	working capital (CA - CL)
NW	=	net worth (TA - TL)
NCE	=	net capital employed (TA - CL)
GDP	=	Gross Domestic Product deflator (1980=100) at T-1
RPI	=	Retail Price Index deflator (1974=100) at T-1
RPI1	=	Retail Price Index deflator (1980=100) at T-2
FA	=	fixed assets (TA - CA)
CAP	=	total nominal value of issued capital
NSP	=	nominal (or par) value of each issued share
NEO	=	number of company employees at T-1
NE1	=	number of company employees at T-2
ER	=	total of all employees' remuneration at T-1
ER1	=	total of all employees' remuneration at T-2
EPS	=	earnings per share at T-1
EPS1	=	earnings per share at T-2

Appendix 2:   Explanatory variables

Key:

A variable followed by 1 refers to T-2, all other variables refer to T-1.

FNF   =   a statistically significant mean difference (at the 5% level or better) between the failed and non-failed samples; with the mean for the non-failed sample being significantly larger - on the basis of a Student's t-test.

FNF*   =   as above, except the sample mean of the failed firms is significantly larger.

NFDA   =   as above, with the mean for the non-failed sample being significantly larger than for the distressed acquired sample.

NFDA* =   as above, except the sample mean of the distressed acquired firms is significantly larger.

FDA   =   as above, with the mean for the distressed acquired sample being significantly larger that for the failed sample.

FDA*   =   as above, except the sample mean of the failed firms is significantly larger.

Dummy/non-financial variables

1. IND   = industry dummy variable; 1 = manufacturing, 0 = non-manufacturing

2. AQGC   = accounts qualified on going concern basis; 1 = qualication, 0 = no qualification: FDA*; FNF*

3. DSSH   = dummy for substantial shareholding (10%+); 1 = substantial shareholding, 0 = no substantial shareholding

4. BS   = number of company directors (board size): FNF; NFDA

5. LAG   = time lag in lunar months (no. days/28) between the financial year end of each company and the date its annual accounts were published: FNF*; NFDA*; FDA*

6. NEO   = number of company employees at T-1: FNF; NFDA

7. NE1   = number of company employees at T-2: FNF; NFDA

8. CNE   = (NEO-NE1)/NE1: FNF*; NFDA*

Financial variables

9. NPTA   = NPBT/TA: NFDA; FNF

10. FFTA   = FF/TA: NFDA; FNF

11. NPNCE   = NPBT/NCE: NFDA

12. FFNCE   = FF/NCE

13. ERD   = (ER/NEO)* RPI: FDA*

14. ERD1   = (ER1/NE1)* RPI1: FDA*

15. REMC   = (ERD-ERD1)/ERD1: NFDA

16. HSP   = (SPH-SPH1)/SPH1: FDA*; FNF*; NFDA*

17. LSP   = (SPL-SPL1)/SPL1: FNF; NFDA

18. SEHSP   = (SEH-SEH1)/SEH1: FNF; NFDA

19. SELSP   = (SEL-SEL1)/SEL1

20. AHSP   = HSP-SEHSP: FDA*; FNF*; NFDA*

21. ALSP   = LSP-SELSP: FNF*

22. STL   = TU/TL: NFDA; FDA; FNF

23. FFTL   = FF/TL: NFDA; FDA; FNF

24. SIZE   = natural log(TA/GDP): NFDA; FNF

25. SIZE1   = natural log(TU*RPI): NFDA; FNF

26. WCTA   = (CA-CL)/TA: NFDA; FNF; FDA*

27. NPCAP = NPBT/CAP: NFDA; FNF

28. FFCAP = FF/CAP: NFDA; FNF

29. TLTA   = TL/TA: NFDA*; FNF*; FDA*

30. CATL   = CA/TL: NFDA; FNF; FDA*

31. CACL   = CA/CL: NFDA; FNF; FDA*

32. NPS   = (NPBT/TU)*100: NFDA; FNF

33. FFS   = (FF/TU)*100: NFDA; FNF

34. TLCAP = TL/(TL+CAP)

35. CLCAP = CL/(CL+CAP)

36. NPFF   = NPBT/FF: NFDA

37. NPCL   = NPBT/CL: NFDA; FNF

38. FFCL   = FF/CL: NFDA; FNF

39. STA   = TU/TA

40. SFA   = S/FA

41. CLTA   = CL/TA: NFDA*; FNF*

42. SSDS   = (SSH+DS)/NS: FNF*

43. DSNS   = DS/NS

44. CWB   = (ER*RPI)-(ER1*RPI1)

45. CDR   = [(DR*RPI)-(DR1*RPI1]/(DR1*RPI1):
             FDA*; NFDA

46. CADR   = CDR/ND

47. DRND   = DR/ND

48. DER   = DR/ER

49. DER1   = DR1/ER1

50. CDER   = DRER-DRER1

171

51. CHLPE   = (SPH/EPS)-(SPL/EPS)

52. CHLPE1   = (SPH1/EPS1)-(SPL1/EPS1): FNF*

53. CCHCPE   = CHLPE-CHLPE1: FNF*

54. CSPL   = (SPL/EPS)-(SPL1/EPS1): FNF*

55. CSPH   = (SPH/EPS)-(SPH1/EPS1): FNF*

56. CCHL   = CSPL-CSPH: FNF*

57. CNS   = NS-NS1: NFDA; FDA*

58. CSH   = (SPH/SEH)-(SPH1/SEH1): FNF*

59. CCL   = CSH-CSL

60. SEHLD   = (SPH/SEH)/(SPL/SEL): FNF*

61. SEHLD1   = (SPH1/SEH1)/(SPL1/SEL1): NFDA*; FNF*

62. ERPI   = ER*RPI: NFDA; FNF

63. ERPI1   = ER*RPI1: NFDA; FNF

64. CERPI   = ERPI-ERPI1

65. SSHN   = SSH/NS

66. EPSD   = EPS*RPI: NFDA; FNF

67. EPSD1   = EPS1*RPI1: NFDA

68. CEPS   = EPSD-EPSD1: NFDA*; FNF*

69. PERA   = ((SPH+SPL)/2)/EPS: NFDA

70. PERA1   = ((SPH1+SPL1)/2)/EPS1

71. CPER   = PERA-PERA1: NFDA*; FNF*

72. MVDR   = [DS*((SPH+SPL)/2)/100]/DR

73. DAE   = (EPSD*NS)+(EPSD1*NS1): FNF; NFDA

74. DNP   = NPBT*RPI: FNF; NFDA

Bibliography

Aldrich, J.H. and Nelson, F.D. (1984), Linear Probability, Logit and Probit Models, Sage Publications.

Allen, M. and Hodgkinson, L. (1986), Buying a Business: A Guide to Decisions, Graham and Trotman.

Altman, E.I. (1968), 'Financial Ratios, Discriminant Analysis and the Prediction of Corporate Bankruptcy', Journal of Finance, vol. 4, no. 4, pp. 589-609.

Altman, E.I. (1970), 'A Reply', Journal of Finance, December, pp. 1169-1172.

Altman, E.I. (1971), Corporate Bankruptcy in America, Heath Lexington Books.

Altman, E.I. (1983), Corporate Financial Distress: A Complete Guide to Predicting, Avoiding and Dealing with Bankruptcy, John Wiley.

Altman, E.I. (1984), 'The Success of Business Failure Prediction Models', Journal of Banking and Finance, vol. 8, no. 1, pp. 171-178.

Amemiya, T. (1981), 'Qualitative Response Models: A Survey', Journal of Economic Literature, December, pp. 1483-1536.

Ang, J. and Chua, J. (1981), 'Corporate Bankruptcy and Job Losses among Top Level Managers', Financial Management, Winter, pp. 70-74.

Ansoff, H.I. (1965), Corporate Strategy: An Analytical Approach to Business Policy for Growth and Expansion, Penguin.

Argenti, J. (1976), Corporate Collapse: The Causes and Symptoms, McGraw-Hill.

Argenti, J. (1983), 'Discerning the Cracks of Company Failure', Director, October, pp. 67-73.

Argenti, J. (1983a), Systematic Corporate Planning, Van Nostrand Reinhold.

Auerbach, A.J. and Reishus, D. (1988), 'The Impact of Taxation on Mergers and Acquisitions', in Mergers and Acquisitions, ed. A.J. Auerbach, University of Chicago Press.

Bank of England (1982), 'Techniques of Assessing Corporate Financial Strength', Bank of England Quarterly Bulletin, vol. 22, no. 2, pp. 221-223.

Barmash, A. (1973), Great Business Disasters, Ballantine Books.

Bathory, A. (1984), Predicting Corporate Collapse: Credit Analysis in the Determination and Forecasting of Insolvent Companies, Financial Times Business Information, London.

Belkaoui, A. (1978), 'Financial Ratios as Predictors of Canadian Takeovers', Journal of Accounting Research, vol. 5, no.1, pp. 93-107.

Blum, M. (1974), 'Failing Company Discriminant Analysis', Journal of Accounting Research, vol. 12, no. 1, pp. 1-25.

Bok, D.C. (1960), 'Section 7 of the Clayton Act and the Merging of Law and Economics', Harvard Law Review, vol. 74, no. 2, pp. 226-356.

Boocock, K. and Drozd, A.F. (1982), 'Forecasting Corporate Collapse: Recognizing the Signs of Bad Times', Chartered Accountants Magazine, November, pp. 54-59.

Boucher, W.I. (1980), The Process of Conglomerate Merger, Federal Trades Commission, Washington.

Bourgeois, L.J. (1981), 'On the Measurement of Organizational Slack', Academy of Management Review, no.6, pp. 29-37.

Boyle, S.E. (1970), 'Profit Characteristics of Large Conglomerate Mergers in The United States, 1948 to 1968', St John's Law Review, Spring, pp. 152-170.

Bozeman, B. and Slusher, E.A. (1979), 'Scarcity and Environmental Stress in Public Organisations', Administration and Society, no. 11, pp. 335-356.

Brown, C. and Medoff, J.L. (1987), The Impact of Firm Acquisition on Labour, DP no. 1327, Institute of Economic Research, Harvard University.

Bruner, R.F. (1988), 'The Use of Excess Cash and Debt Capacity as a Motive for Merger', Journal of Financial and Quantitative Analysis, vol. 23, no. 7, pp. 199-217.

Buona, A.F. and Bowditch, J.L. (1989), The Human Side of Mergers and Acquisitions, Jossey-Bass Publishers.

Carleton, W.T., Guilkey, D.K., Harris, R.S. and Stewart, J.F. (1983), 'An Empirical Analysis of the Role of the Medium of Exchange in Mergers', Journal of Finance, June, pp. 249-262.

Casey, C.J., McGee, V.E. and Stickney, C.P. (1986), 'Discriminating between Reorganized and Liquidated Firms in Bankruptcy', Accounting Review, no. 2, pp. 813-826.

Chambers, P. (1985), 'Turning Loss to Profit: Fire the Top Brass', Works Management, October, pp. 20-25.

Chapman, D.R. and Junor, C.W. (1987), 'Inflation, Firm Control Type and Vulnerability to Takeover', Oxford Economic Papers, no. 39, pp. 500-525.

Clarke, T. and Weinstein, M. (1987), 'The Behaviour of the Common Stock of Bankrupt Firms', Journal of Finance, May, pp. 489-506.

Cohen, R.L. (1973), 'Confidence Comes before a Crash', Business Administration, January, pp. 10-15.

Conn, R.L. (1976), 'The Failing Firm/Industry Doctrines in Conglomerate Mergers', Journal of Industrial Economics, vol. 25, pp. 181-187.

Cook, T.E. (1986), Mergers and Acquisitions, Basil Blackwell.

Copeland, T.E. and Weston, J.F. (1983), Financial Theory and Corporate Policy, Addison Wesley.

Copp, P. (1987), 'Insolvency Buyouts', Business Graduate Journal, October, pp. 3-4.

Cosh, A., Hughes, A. and Singh, A. (1984), The Causes and Effects of Takeovers: An Empirical Investigation, ER no. 87, Department of Applied Economics, University of Cambridge.

Cyert, R.M. and March, J.G. (1963), A Behavioural Theory of the Firm, Prentice-Hall.

Dambolena, I.G. (1983), 'The Prediction of Corporate Failure', Omega (International Journal of Management Science), vol. 11, no. 4, pp. 355-364.

DeAngelo, H., DeAngelo, E. and Rice, M. (1984), 'Going Private: Minority Freezeouts and Stockholder Wealth', Journal of Law and Economics, October, pp. 367-401.

Dewey, D. (1961), 'Mergers and Cartels: Some Reservations about Policy', American Economic Review, vol. 51, pp. 255-262.

Dewing, A.S. (1941), The Financial Policy of Corporations, Ronald Press.

Drucker, P.F. (1981), 'The Five Rules of Successful Acquisition', Wall Street Journal, October, p. 28.

Efron, B. (1978), 'Regression and Anova with Zero-one Data: Measures of Residual Variation',

Journal of American Statistical Association, March, pp. 872-898.

El Hennawy and Morris, R.C. (1983), 'Market Anticipation of Corporate Failure in the UK', Journal of Business Finance and Accounting, vol. 5, no. 1, pp. 359-372.

El Hennawy and Morris, R.C. (1983a), 'The Significance of the Base Year in Developing Failure Prediction Models', Journal of Business Finance and Accounting, vol. 5, no. 1, pp. 209-223.

Fairburn, J.A. and Kay, J.A. (1989), Mergers and Merger Policy, eds., Oxford University Press.

Finkin, E.F. (1987), Successful Corporate Turnarounds, Quorum Books.

Franks, J., Harris, R. and Mayer, C. (1987), Means of Payment in Takeover: Results for the UK and US, DP no. 200, Centre for Economic Policy Research, London.

George, P.B.S. (1986), 'The Emergence of the Public Company Management Buy-out', Acquisitions Monthly, March, pp. 44-48.

Gort, M. (1969), 'An Economic Disturbance Theory of Mergers', Quarterly Journal of Economics, no. 83, pp. 624-642.

Grammatikos, T., Makhija, A.K. and Thompson, H.E. (1988), 'Financing Corporate Takeover by Individuals Seeking Control, Managerial and Decision Economics, vol. 9, pp. 227-235.

Green, S. (1988), 'The Incentive Effects of Ownership and Control in Management Buyouts', Long Range Planning, no. 1, pp. 26-34.

Guardian (1987), 'Murdoch Wins Approval for Today Takeover', The Guardian, 2 July.

Guth, W.D. (1985), 'Corporate Growth Strategies', Journal of Business Strategy, no. 2, pp. 64-72.

Hall, P.D. and Norburn, D. (1987), 'The Management Factor in Acquisition Performance', Leadership and

Organisation Development Journal, no. 3, pp. 23-30.

Hambrick, D.C. and D'Aventi, R.A. (1988), 'Large Corporate Failures as Downward Spirals', Administrative Science Quarterly, no. 33, pp. 1-23.

Hambrick, D.C. and Schecter, S.M. (1983), 'Turnaround Strategies in Mature Industrial-Product Business Units', Academy of Management Journal, vol. 26, no. 2, pp. 231-248.

Hannan, M.T. and Freeman, J.H. (1984), 'Structural Intertia and Organizational Change', American Sociological Review, no. 49, pp. 149-164.

Hanushek, E.A. (1977), 'Models with Discrete Dependent Variables', in Statistical Methods for Social Scientists, New York Academic Press.

Harrigan, K.R. (1980), Strategies for Declining Industries, Lexington MA: Heath.

Harvey, J.L. and Newgarden, A. (1965), 'Planning for Mergers and Acquisitions', in Management Guides to Mergers and Acquisitions, John Wiley.

Hofer, C.W. (1980), 'Turnaround Strategies', Journal of Business Strategy, no. 1, pp. 19-31.

Holl, P. and Pickering, J.F. (1988), The Determinants and Effects of Actual, Abandoned and Contested Mergers', Managerial and Decision Economics, vol. 9, pp. 1-19.

Homan, M. (1984), 'Insolvency: Spotting the Danger Signals', Banking World, October, pp. 33-39.

Hudson, J. (1987), 'The Age, Regional and Industrial Structure of Company Liquidations', Journal of Business Finance and Accounting, vol. 14, no. 2, pp. 200-213.

Hughes, A. (1987), The Impact of Mergers: A Survey of Empirical Evidence, Department of Applied Economics Working Paper, University of Cambridge.

Hughes, A., Mueller, D.C. and Singh, A. (1984), Hypotheses about Mergers, ER no. 85, Department of

Applied Economics, University of Cambridge.

Hunt, J. (1988), 'Managing the Successful Acquisition: A People Question', London Business School Journal, vol. 12, no. 1, pp. 2-15.

Hunt, J. and Lees, S. (1987), 'The Predator Myth', Management Today, November, pp. 116-121.

Jensen, M.C. (1986), 'Agency Costs of Free Cash Flows, Corporate Finance and Takeovers', American Economic Review, May, pp. 323-329.

Jensen, M.C. and Meckling, W.H. (1976), 'Theory of the Firm, Managerial Behaviour, Agency Costs and Ownership Structure', Journal of Financial Economics, October, pp. 305-333.

Jensen, M.C. and Ruback, R.S. (1983), 'The Market for Corporate Control', Journal of Financial Economics, April, pp. 5-50.

John, D. (1988), 'Sound Diffusion Call in Receiver', The Guardian, 6 December.

Johnson, G.C. (1970), 'Ratio Analysis and the Prediction of Firm Failure', Journal of Finance, December, pp. 1166-1168.

Johnson, G. and Scholes, K. (1984), Exploring Corporate Strategy, Prentice Hall.

Keasey, K. and Watson, R. (1987), 'Non-financial Symptoms and the Prediction of Small Company Failure: A Test of Argenti's Hypotheses', Journal of Business Finance and Accounting, vol. 14, no. 3, pp. 335-354.

Kharbanda, O.P. and Stallworthy, E.A. (1985), Corporate Failure: Prediction, Panacea and Prevention, McGraw-Hill.

Kharbanda, O.P. and Stallworthy, E.A. (1987), Company Rescue: How to Manage a Company Turnaround, Heinemann.

Kibel, H.R. (1982), How to Turn Around a Financially Troubled Company, McGraw-Hill.

Klecka, W.R. (1980), Discriminant Analysis, Sage

Publications.

LBS (1987), A Study to Determine the Reasons for Failure of Small Businesses in the UK, London Business School, Stoy Hayward/National Westminster Bank PLC, London.

Lee, T.A. (1986), Company Auditing, Gee Books.

Lee, W.Y. and Barker, H.H. (1977), 'Bankruptcy Costs and the Firm's Optimal Debt Capacity: A Positive Theory of Capital Structure', Southern Economic Journal, vol. 43, pp. 1453-1465.

Lewellen, W. (1977), 'A Pure Financial Rationale for the Conglomerate Merger', Journal of Finance, vol. 26, pp. 521-537.

Lincoln, M. (1984), 'An Empirical Study of the Usefulness of Accounting Ratios to Describe Levels of Insolvency Risk', Journal of Banking and Finance, vol. 8, no. 1, pp. 321-340.

Lintner, J. (1971), 'Expectations, Mergers and Equilibrium in Purely Competitive Securities Markets', American Economic Review, May, pp. 101-111.

Lo, A.W. (1986), 'Logit versus Discriminant Analysis: A Specification Test and Application to Corporate Bankruptcies', Journal of Econmetrics, no. 31, pp. 151-178.

Maddala, G.S. (1983), Limited Dependent and Qualitative Variables in Econometrics, Cambridge University Press.

Mandelker, G. (1974), 'Risk and Return: The Case of Merging Firms', Journal of Financial Economics, no. 1, pp. 303-333.

Manne, H.G. (1965), 'Mergers and the Market for Corporate Control', Journal of Political Economy, no. 73, pp. 110-119.

Marias, D.A.J. (1979), A Method of Quantifying Companies Relative Financial Strength, Bank of England DP no. 4, London.

Maupin, R.J. (1987), 'Financial and Stock Market

Variables as Predictors of Management Buyouts', *Strategic Management Journal*, vol. 8, pp. 319-327.

McFadden, D. (1973), 'Conditional Logit Analysis of Qualitative Choice Behaviour', in *Frontiers in Econometrics*, ed. P. Zarembka, Academic Press.

McMillan, E.M. (1984), 'Anticipating Failure: Reading the Early Warning Signals', *Hong Kong Manager*, July, pp. 7-14.

Meeks, G. (1977), *Disappointing Marriage: A Study of the Gains from Mergers*, Cambridge University Press.

Miller, D. and Friesen, P.H. (1977), 'Strategy-making in Context: Ten Empirical Archetypes', *Journal of Management Studies*, no. 14, pp. 253-280.

Mueller, D.C. (1977), 'The Effects of Conglomerate Mergers: A Survey of the Empirical Facts', *Journal of Banking and Finance*, vol. 1, pp. 315-374.

Mueller, D.C. (1980), 'Mergers in the United States, 1962 to 1972', in *The Determinants and Effects of Mergers*, ed. D.C. Mueller, Cambridge: Oelgeschlayer, Gunn and Hain.

Mutchler, J.F. (1984), 'Auditors' Perceptions of the Going Concern Opinion Decision', *Auditing: A Journal of Practice and Theory*, vol. 3, no. 2, pp. 17-29.

Myers, S.C. and Majluf, N.S. (1984), 'Corporate Financing and Investment Decisions when Firms have Information that Investors do not have', *Journal of Financial Economics*, June, pp. 187-223.

Napier, N.K. (1989), 'Merger and Acquisition Human Resources Issues and Outcomes: A Review and Suggested Typology', *Journal of Management Studies*, vol. 26, no. 3, pp. 271-290.

Newbould, G.D. (1970), *Management and Merger Activity*, Guthstead.

Newbould, G.D. (1970a), *Business Finance*, George G. Harris.

Norgard, R. (1987), 'Forecasting Corporate Failure', The Chartered Accountant in Australia, August, pp. 44-46.

Norusis, C.M.J. (1985), Advanced Statistical Guide: SPSSX, McGraw-Hill.

Oates, D. (1987), 'Industrial Rescue', Director, September, pp. 23-24.

OECD (1974), Mergers and Competition Policy, OECD, Paris.

OFT (1985), Mergers: A Guide to the Procedures under the Fair Trading Act 1973, HMSO, London.

Ohlson, J.A. (1980), 'Financial Ratios and the Probabilistic Prediction of Bankruptcy', Journal of Accounting Research, vol. 15, no. 1, pp. 109-131.

Palepu, K.G. (1986), 'Predicting Takeover Targets: A Methodological and Empirical Analysis', Journal of Accounting and Economics, no. 8, pp. 3-25.

Pastena, V. and Ruland, W. (1986), 'The Merger/Bankruptcy Alternative', Accounting Review, no. 2, pp. 288-301.

Peel, M.J. (1985), 'Directors' Shareholdings in Failed Companies and Insider Dealing Controls', Investment Analyst, no. 77, pp. 17-23.

Peel, M.J. (1985a), Timeliness of Accounting Reports and Predicting Corporate Failure: A Logistic Analysis, DP no. 54, Department of Economic and Business Studies, University of Liverpool.

Peel, M.J. (1987), 'Timeliness of Private Company Accounts and Predicting Corporate Failure', Investment Analyst, no. 83, pp. 23-27.

Peel, M.J. (1989), 'The Going Concern Qualification Debate: Some UK Evidence', British Accounting Review, vol. 23, no. 1, pp. 1-24.

Peel, M.J. and Peel, D.A. (1987), 'Some Further Empirical Evidence on Predicting Private Company Failure', Accounting and Business Research, no. 69, pp. 57-66.

Peel, M.J. and Peel, D.A. (1988), 'A Multilogit Approach to Predicting Corporate Failure - Some Evidence for the UK Corporate Sector', Omega (International Journal of Management Science), vol. 16, no. 4, pp. 309-318.

Peel, M.J., Peel, D.A. and Pope, P.F. (1985), 'Some Evidence on Corporate Failure and the Behaviour of Non-financial Ratios', Investment Analyst, no. 75, pp. 3-7.

Peel, M.J., Peel, D.A. and Pope, P.F. (1986), 'Predicting Corporate Failure: Some Results for the UK Corporate Sector', Omega (International Journal of Management Science), vol. 14, no. 1, pp. 5-12.

Peel, D.A. and Pope, P.F. (1984), 'Corporate Accounting Data, Capital Market Information and Wage Increases of the Firm', Journal of Business Finance and Accounting, vol. 11, no. 2, pp. 177-188.

Pekar, P. (1985), 'A Strategic Approach to Diversification', Journal of Business Strategy, no. 4, pp. 84-95.

Pope, P.F., Morris, R.C. and Peel, D.A. (1988), Failure Prediction Models: A Review and an Experiment, Mimeo, Department of Accounting, University of Strathclyde.

Questat (1984), Qualitative Response Model Estimation and Statistics, by B. Knox and S. Missiakoulis, PSSRU, University of Kent.

Ravenscraft, D.J. and Scherer, F.M. (1987), 'Life after Takeover', Journal of Industrial Economics, December, pp. 147-156.

Ravenscraft, D.J. and Scherer, F.M. (1987a), Mergers, Sell-offs, and Economic Efficiency, The Brookings Institution.

Rege, U.P. (1984), 'Accounting Ratios to Locate Takeover Targets', Journal of Business Finance and Accounting, vol. 11, no. 3, pp. 301-311.

Robbie, K. (1988), 'Management Buyouts', British Business, January, pp. 20-21.

Ross, J.E. and Kami, M.J. (1973), Corporate Management in Crisis, Prentice-Hall.

Schendel, D., Patton, G.R. and Riggs, J.C. (1976), 'Corporate Turnaround Strategies', Journal of General Management, vol. 3. no. 3, pp. 3-11.

Scott, J. (1977), 'On the Theory of Conglomerate Mergers', Journal of Finance, vol. 32, pp. 1235-1250.

Scott, J. (1981), 'The Probability of Bankruptcy: A Comparison of Empirical Predictions and Theoretical Models', Journal of Banking and Finance, vol. 5, no. 3, pp. 317-344.

Shazam (1982), Shazam - An Econometrics Computer Program: Version 4.3, by K.J. White, Department of Economics, University of British Columbia.

Shelton, L.M. (1988), 'Strategic Business Fits and Corporate Acquisition: Empirical Evidence', Strategic Management Journal, vol. 9, pp. 279-287.

Shleifer, A., Vishny, R.N. and Morck, P. (1987), Characteristics of Hostile and Friendly Takeover Targets, WP 213, Centre for Research in Security Prices, University of Chicago.

Shrieves, R.E. and Stevens, D.L. (1979), 'Bankruptcy Avoidance as a Motive for Mergers', Journal of Financial and Quantitative Analysis, no. 3, pp. 501-515.

Singh, J.V. (1986), 'Performance, Slack and Risk-taking in Organisation Decision-making', Academy of Management Journal, no. 29, pp. 562-585.

Slatter, S. (1984), Corporate Recovery: Successful Turnaround Strategies and their Implementation, Penguin.

Smith, R.A. (1966), Corporations in Crises, Doubleday.

Sotiroff, P. (1963), 'Federal Antitrust Laws and Mergers: An Updating of the Failing Company Doctrine', Michigan Law Review, vol. 61, no. 3, pp. 566-583.

SPSS (1975), Statistical Package for the Social Sciences, McGraw-Hill.

Staw, B.M., Sandelands, L.E. and Dutton, J.E. (1981), 'Threat-rigidity Effects in Organizational Behaviour: A Multi-level Analysis', Administrative Science Quarterly, no. 26, pp. 501-524.

Steiner, G.A. (1969), Top Management Planning, MacMillan.

Stevens, D.L. (1973), 'Financial Characteristics of Merged Firms: A Multivariate Analysis', Journal of Financial and Quantitative Analysis, March, pp. 149-158.

Storey, D., Keasey, K., Watson, R. and Wynarczyk, P. (1987), The Performance of Small Firms, Croom Helm.

Taffler, R.J. (1983), 'The Assessment of Company Solvency and Performance Using a Statistical Model', Accounting and Business Research, vol. 15, no. 52, pp. 295-308.

Taffler, R.J. (1984), 'Empirical Models for the Monitoring of UK Corporations', Journal of Banking and Finance, vol. 8, pp. 199-227.

Taffler, R.J. and Holl, P. (1988), Abandoned Mergers and the Market for Corporate Control, Industrial and Labour Economics Research Unit, The City University, London.

Taffler, R.J. and Tseung, M. (1984), 'The Audited Going Concern Qualification in Practice: Exploring Some Myths', The Accountants Magazine, July, pp. 263-269.

Taylor, B. (1983), 'Turnaround, Recovery and Growth: the Way through the Crises', Journal of General Management, vol. 8, no.2, pp. 5-13.

Tisshaw, H.J. (1976), Evaluation of Downside Risk Using Financial Ratios, unpublished MSc thesis, City University Business School, London.

Tushman, M.L. and Anderson, P.C. (1986), 'Technological Discontinuities and Organizational

Environments', Administrative Science Quarterly, no. 31, pp. 439-459.

Tweedie, D. (1989), Creative Accounting and Current Financial Reporting Developments, paper given at BAA Annual Conference, March, University of Bath.

Vance, S.C. (1971), Managers in the Conglomerate Era, Wiley-Interscience.

Varaiya, N.P. (1988), 'The Winner's Curse Hypothesis and Corporate Takeovers', Managerial and Decision Economics, no. 9, pp. 209-219.

Wadhwani, S.B. (1984), Inflation, Bankruptcy, Default Premia and the Stock Market, DP no. 194, Centre for Labour Economics, London School of Economics.

Walsh, J.P. (1988), 'Top Management Turnover following Mergers and Acquisitions', Strategic Management Journal, vol. 9, pp. 173-183.

Weston, J.F. and Mansinghka, S.K. (1971), 'Tests of Efficiency Performance in Conglomerate Firms', Journal of Finance, September, pp. 919-936.

Wright, M. and Coyne, J. (1985), Management Buyouts, Croom Helm.

Wright, M., Coyne, J. and Mills, A. (1987), Spicer and Pegler's Management Buyouts, Woodhead-Faulkner, Cambridge.

Zavgren, C.V. (1985), 'Assessing the Vulnerability to Failure of American Industrial Firms: A Logistic Analysis', Journal of Business Finance and Accounting, vol. 12, no. 1, pp. 19-45.

Index

191